Ready® Common Core

Mathematics Instruction ❶

Curriculum Associates

Project Manager: Cynthia Tripp
Cover Designer and Illustrator: Julia Bourque
Illustrator: Sam Valentino
Book Design: Scott Hoffman

ISBN 978-0-7609-8855-8
©2014—Curriculum Associates, LLC
North Billerica, MA 01862

Table of Contents

Table of Contents

Unit 1 – Operations and Algebraic Thinking
Add and Subtract

6 balloon stickers and 3 star stickers. Lee wants to share some stickers. He wants some stickers for his notebook. What math questions could Lee ask about the stickers?

In this unit you will learn ways to add and subtract. Then you will be able to solve problems like Lee's!

✓ **Self Check** ·

Check off the skills you know now. Then see how many more you can check off after each lesson!

I can:	Before this unit	After this unit
count on to add.	☐	☐
count on to subtract.	☐	☐
solve addition and subtraction word problems.	☐	☐
use addition sentences to write subtraction sentences.	☐	☐
find missing addends.	☐	☐
subtract to compare.	☐	☐

A team has 5 girls and 3 boys.
How many children are on the team in all?

 **Model It** **Find 5 + 3.** ●

One part shows girls. One part shows boys.
Count on from 5 to **add** girls and boys.

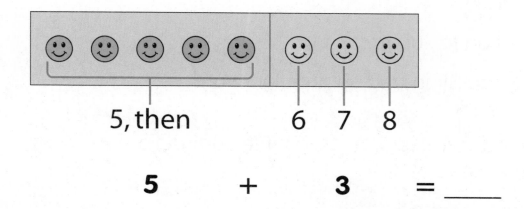

5, then   6 7 8

5   **+**   **3**   **=** ____

Learn Together
Count On to Add

6 blocks are yellow. 2 blocks are red.
How many blocks in all?
How do you know?

 Model It Find 6 + 2.

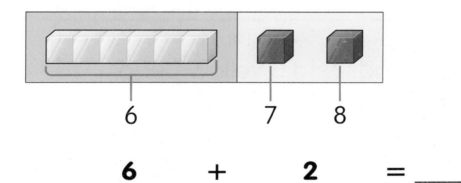

6   7   8

6   +   2   = ____

Talk About It What is wrong?

6 blocks are yellow. 3 blocks are red.
How many blocks in all?
What's wrong?

1, then   2,   3,   4

▶ Show the right way.   ____, then ____, ____, ____

6   +   3   = ____

Practice Together
Count On to Add

5 red markers and 3 blue markers.
How many markers in all?

5 + 3 = ___8___

5 red

6   7   8

---

1 6 red beads and 3 yellow beads.
How many beads in all?

6 + 3 = _____

---

2 6 red blocks and 2 blue blocks.
How many blocks in all?

6 + 2 = _____

6

Practice by Myself
Count On to Add

3   5 big balls and 3 small balls.
How many balls in all?

5 + 3 = ____

4   1 bee and 7 ants.
How many bugs in all?

1 + 7 = ____

5   6 triangles and 2 squares.
How many shapes in all?

____ = 6 + 2

6 children play ball. 4 go home early.
How many children are left?

Model It Find 6 – 4. ●

Start with the number of children who leave.

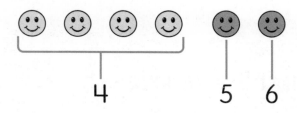

4   5   6

Start at 4.   Count on to 6.
                          Count on ___2___.

6 – 4 = ____

Count On to Subtract

There are 7 bikes. 4 are red.
The rest are black.

How many are black?
How can you find out?

Model It   **Find 7 − 4.**

Start at 4.   Count on to 7.

$$7 - 4 = \underline{\quad} \qquad 4 + \underline{\quad} = 7$$

Talk About It   **Who is right? How do you know?**

There are 8 children. 5 are boys. How many are girls?

Buzz: Boom:

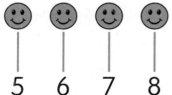
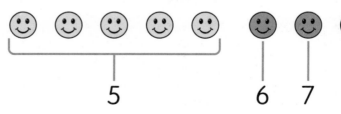

$$8 - 5 = 4 \qquad\qquad 8 - 5 = 3$$

Count On to Subtract

Ali has 7 markers. Some are blue.

5 are red.

How many are blue?

$7 - 5 = ?$

$5 + \underline{\;2\;} = 7$

5 red

6 7

---

1 There are 8 cups. 5 are big. The rest are small.
How many are small?

$8 - 5 = \underline{\qquad}$ $8 = \underline{\qquad} + 5$

---

2 There are 9 balloons. 6 balloons pop.
How many balloons are left?

1 2 3 4 5 ⑥ 7 8 9 10

$9 - 6 = \underline{\qquad}$ $6 + 3 = \underline{\qquad}$

Count On to Subtract

3 Jen has 8 buttons. 6 are square.

The rest are round. How many buttons are round?

$8 - 6 =$ _____ $6 +$ _____ $= 8$

4 6 fish are in the weeds. 3 swim away.

How many are left?

| 1 | 2 | 3 | 4 | 5 | 6 | 7 | 8 | 9 | 10 |

$6 - 3 =$ _____ $6 = 3 +$ _____

5 6 flowers are in a vase.

5 flowers are short.

The rest are tall.

How many flowers are tall?

$6 - 5 =$ _____ $5 +$ _____ $= 6$

Add and Subtract in Word Problems

3 children are sitting.

More children sit down.

Now there are 5 children.

How many more children sit down?

Model It Find **3 + ____ = 5.** ....

Start with 3. Count on.

How many more make 5?

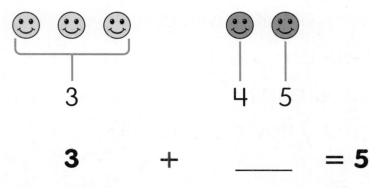

3 + ____ = **5**

____ more children sit down.

Learn Together
Add and Subtract in Word Problems

Jan has 6 pencils.
She gives some away.
Now she has 5 pencils.
How many does she give away?

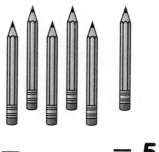

6   –   _____ = 5

Model It   **Find 6 – _____ = 5.** •

Start with 5. How many more makes 6?

5   +   _____ = 6

6   –   _____ = 5

Jan gives away _____ pencil(s).

Talk About It   **Who is right? How do you know?** • • • • • • • • • • • •

There are 8 pencils.
4 are yellow. The rest are blue.
How many are blue?

Buzz: **4   +   8   = ?**   Boom: **4   +   ?   = 8**

Practice Together
Add and Subtract in Word Problems

There are 8 frogs. Some are big.

5 are small.

How many are big?

Count on __3__ .

4 (5) 6 7 8 9

8 − __3__ = 5

__3__ frogs are big.

1 Greg has 8 toys. He puts some away.

Now there are 6 toys.

How many toys are put away?

8 − ____ = 6

____ toys are put away.

2 There are 7 balls. 5 are soccer balls.

The rest are kickballs.

How many kickballs are there?

____ + 5 = 7

There are ____ kickballs.

Practice by Myself
Add and Subtract in Word Problems

3 Emma has 3 beads. She gets more beads.

Now she has 6.

How many new beads does she get?

3 + ___ = 6

Emma gets ___ new beads.

4 9 kites are flying. Some fall.

Now there are 7 kites.

How many kites fall?

9 − ___ = 7

___ kites fall.

5 Jimmy picks 7 peppers. 5 are green.

The rest are red.

How many peppers are red?

5 + ___ = 7

___ peppers are red.

Understand
Missing Addends

How can adding help you subtract?

$5 - 4 = ?$

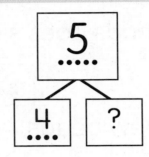

Think   **What are the two parts?** ·

Which number bond shows $5 - 4$? Circle.

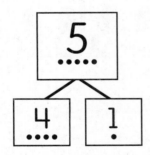

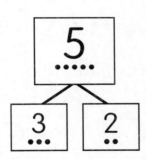

Talk About It ·

What addition sentence helps you find $5 - 4$?

Understand Missing Addends

 Find 7 − 3.

Use 7 counters. → Put the rest in → Write the
Keep 3.   a cup.   answer.

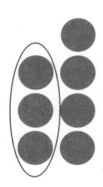

$3 + \underline{4} = 7$

$7 - 3 = \underline{4}$

---

1 Find 7 − 5.

Draw and write.

$5 + \underline{} = 7$

$7 - 5 = \underline{}$

2 Find 7 − 4.

Draw and write.

$4 + \underline{} = 7$

$7 - 4 = \underline{}$

 **Talk About It** •

How can you add to find 6 − 4?

Connect It
Understand Missing Addends

3 **Show** Write a subtraction sentence.
Then write an addition sentence.

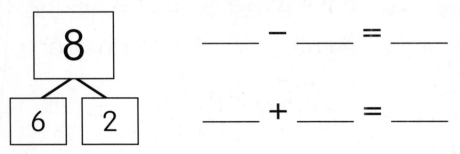

___ − ___ = ___

___ + ___ = ___

4 **Reason** There are 8 cats. 5 are black.
The rest are gray. How many are gray?

Show how you solve.

5 **Explain** There are 5 beads. 4 are on the table.
The rest are in a cup.

▸ Buzz says there are 9 beads in the cup.

▸ Do you agree? Why? Why not?

Understand Missing Addends

6 **Think about missing addends.**

   A: Color some triangles red and some blue.
   Complete the number bond. Write a subtraction
   and an addition sentence.

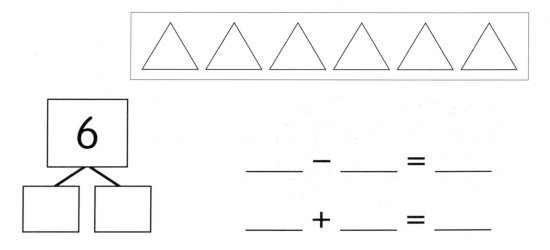

___ − ___ = ___

___ + ___ = ___

   B: Color a different number of triangles red and blue.
   Complete the number bond. Write a subtraction
   and an addition sentence.

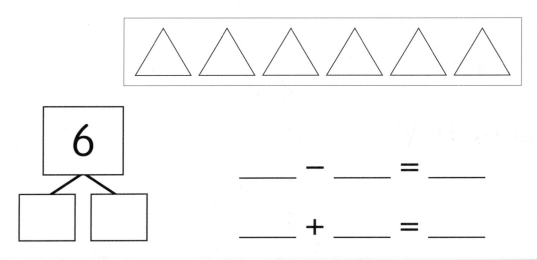

___ − ___ = ___

___ + ___ = ___

There are 6 children. There are 4 hats.

Are there **more** hats or children?

How many children do not get a hat?

Model It Find 6 – 4. •••••••••••••••••••••••••••••••••••••

Match 4 hats with 4 children.

4 and how many more make 6?

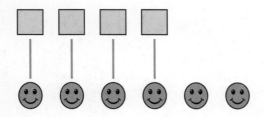

$$6 - 4 = \rule{2cm}{0.4pt}$$

_____ children do not get a hat.

Subtract to Compare in Word Problems

There are 5 pieces of cheese and 8 mice.

Are there **fewer** mice or pieces of cheese?

How many mice do not get cheese?

Model It Find 8 − 5.

Start with 5.

5 and how many more make 8?

8 − 5 = _____

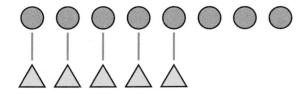

Talk About It Who is right? How do you know?

How many fewer sticks than skates
are there?

Buzz says there are 3 fewer sticks.

Boom says there is 1 fewer stick.

Practice Together
Subtract to Compare in Word Problems

Nan sees 6 birds. Cam sees 9 birds.
How many fewer birds does Nan see?

9 − 6 = __3__

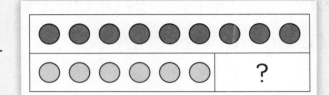

Nan sees __3__ fewer birds.

---

1   4 red markers and 7 blue markers.
How many more blue markers are there?

7 − 4 = ____

____ more blue markers

---

2   8 apples and 6 bananas.
How many more apples
are there?

____ more apples

Subtract to Compare in Word Problems

3 Jo has 7 fish. Pat has 6 fish.
How many more fish does Jo have?

7 – ＿＿ = 6

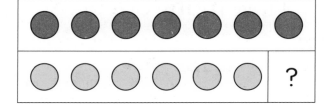

Jo has ＿＿ more fish.

4 7 big shells and 9 small shells.
How many more small shells are there?

9 – ＿＿ = ＿＿

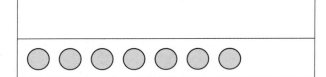

＿＿ more small shells

5 5 chairs and 6 desks.
How many fewer chairs are there?

6 – ＿＿ = ＿＿

＿＿ fewer chair(s)

Unit 1 Review

Solve the problems.

1 8 blocks in all. 6 are red.
Some are blue.
How many are blue?

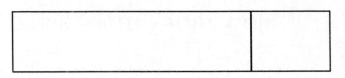

$8 - \underline{} = 6$

---

2 5 children play. 3 more children come.
How many children in all?

1	2	3	4	5	6	7	8	9	10

$\underline{} = 5 + 3$

---

3 $7 - 2 = \underline{}$

4 $6 + 3 = \underline{}$

---

5 $\underline{} = 9 - 2$

6 $6 + 1 = \underline{}$

7 6 birds and 3 ants. How many more birds are there than ants?

Draw a picture that shows the problem.
Then write a number sentence.

_____ − _____ = _____

There are _____ more birds than ants.

---

8 9 buttons in all.
7 are square. Some are round.
How many are round?

Complete the number bond.
Write an addition sentence.
Then write a subtraction sentence.

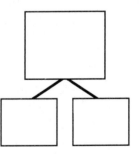

_____ + _____ = _____   _____ − _____ = _____

There are _____ round buttons.

Put It Together

9 **Draw a picture to show an addition story problem.**

Use the numbers 7, 5, and 2.
Tell or write your addition problem.
Write the addition sentence.

_____ + _____ = _____

 3 red flowers and 3 blue flowers. 5 yellow flowers and 4 pink flowers. Beth wants to draw pictures of the some of the flowers. What math questions could Beth ask about the flowers?

In this unit, you will learn different ways to make and add numbers to 10. Then you will be able to solve problems like Beth's.

✓ Self Check

Check off the skills you know now. Then see how many more you can check off after each lesson!

I can:	Before this unit	After this unit
use doubles and doubles plus 1 to add.	☐	☐
find number partners for 6 and 7.	☐	☐
find number partners for 8 and 9.	☐	☐
find number partners for 10.	☐	☐
tell the meaning of the equal sign (=).	☐	☐
tell if a number sentence is true or untrue.	☐	☐
add numbers with totals to 10.	☐	☐

3 players pass a ball.

3 players trap a ball.

How many players in all?

Model It   Find 3 + 3.

Each addend is 3.

Use **doubles** to find the total.

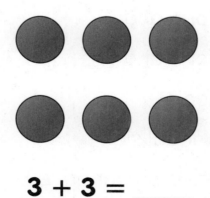

3 + 3 = _____

Doubles and Doubles Plus 1

3 players on the blue team. 4 players on the red team.
How many players in all?

Model It Use doubles. Add 1 more. · · · · · · · · · · · · · · · · · ·

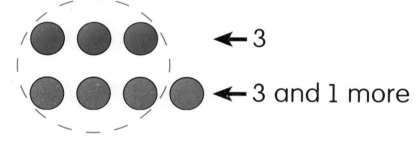

← 3

← 3 and 1 more

$$3 + 3 + 1 = \underline{\quad}$$

$$3 + 4 = \underline{\quad}$$

Talk About It Who is right? How do you know? · · · · · · · · · ·

Boom wrote: **4 + 4 + 1**.

Buzz wrote: **5 + 5 − 1**.

Practice Together
Doubles and Doubles Plus 1

2 red blocks and 3 blue blocks.
How many blocks in all?

$2 + 2 + 1 = \underline{5}$

$2 + \quad 3 \quad = \underline{5}$

← 2
← 2 + 1

1 There are 4 balls. 2 are big. The rest are small.
How many balls are small?

$2 + \underline{\quad} = 4$

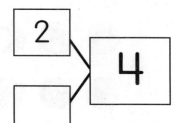

2 Jo has 4 pencils. She finds 3 more pencils.
How many pencils does Jo have in all?

$3 + 3 + \underline{\quad} = \underline{\quad}$

$3 + 4 = \underline{\quad}$

Practice by Myself
Doubles and Doubles Plus 1

3   2 books and 3 books

How many books in all?

____ + ____ + ____ = ____

2 + 3 = ____

---

4   There are 4 birds. More birds join them.

Now there are 8 birds.

How many birds join?

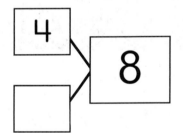

4 + ____ = 8

---

5   Nick has 5 sun stickers.

He has 5 moon stickers.

How many stickers does Nick have in all?

5 + 5 = ____

A quilt has 6 squares in a row.
Some are blue. Some are green.
What are all the ways to make 6?

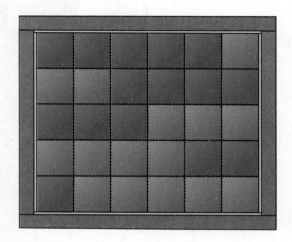

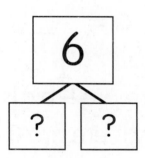

Model It **Find the ways to make 6.** •

$1 + \underline{\hspace{0.3cm} 5 \hspace{0.3cm}} = 6$

$2 + \underline{\hspace{0.8cm}} = 6$

$3 + \underline{\hspace{0.8cm}} = 6$

Number Partners for 6 and 7

A painting has 7 circles in a row.

Some are purple. Some are orange.

What are all the ways to make 7?

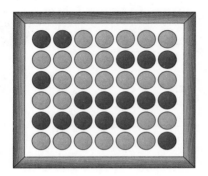

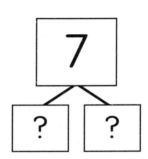

Model It **Find the ways to make 7.**

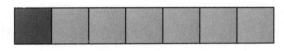

$$1 + \underline{\hspace{1cm}} = 7$$

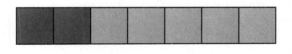

$$2 + \underline{\hspace{1cm}} = 7$$

$$3 + \underline{\hspace{1cm}} = 7$$

Talk About It **Who is right? How do you know?**

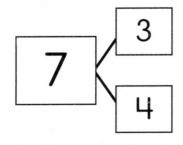

Boom writes: $3 + 4 = 7$.

Buzz writes: $4 = 7 - 3$.

Practice Together
Number Partners for 6 and 7

Write four number sentences.

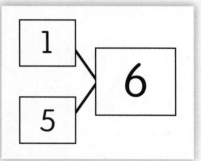

$6 = \underline{1} + \underline{5}$

$6 = \underline{5} + \underline{1}$

$6 - \underline{1} = \underline{5}$

$6 - \underline{5} = \underline{1}$

1 Complete the number bond.
Write two addition sentences.

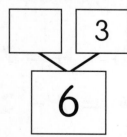

$7 = \underline{} + \underline{}$

$7 = \underline{} + \underline{}$

2 Complete the number bond.
Write a subtraction sentence.

$3 = 6 - \underline{}$

Number Partners for 6 and 7

3 Complete the number bond.
Write two subtraction sentences.

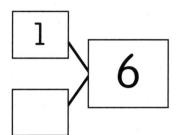

6 – _____ = _____

_____ = 6 – _____

4 Complete the number bond.
Write two addition sentences.

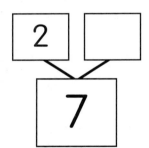

7 = _____ + _____

_____ + _____ = 7

5 Complete the number bond.
Write four number sentences.

7

6

_____ + _____ = 7   7 – _____ = _____

7 = _____ + _____   _____ = 7 – _____

Ed rolls two number cubes.

He adds to get 8.

What are all the ways to make 8?

 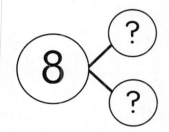

Model It **Find the ways to make 8.** •

1 + _7_ = 8   ___ + 1 = 8

2 + _6_ = 8   ___ + 2 = 8

3 + _5_ = 8   ___ + 3 = 8

4 + _4_ = 8

Number Partners for 8 and 9

A teacher makes groups of 9 children.
Some are girls. Some are boys.
What are all the ways to make 9?

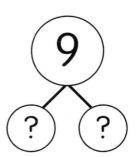

Model It Find the ways to make 9. •

$1 + \underline{\quad} = 9$ $\qquad \underline{\quad} + 1 = 9$

$2 + \underline{\quad} = 9$ $\qquad \underline{\quad} + 2 = 9$

$3 + \underline{\quad} = 9$ $\qquad \underline{\quad} + 3 = 9$

$4 + \underline{\quad} = 9$ $\qquad \underline{\quad} + 4 = 9$

Talk About It Do you agree? Why or why not? • • • • • • • • • •

Buzz says that 0 and 9
are partners of 9.

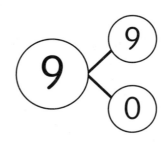

Number Partners for 8 and 9

Write four number sentences.

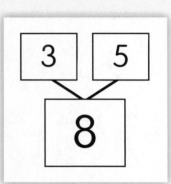

$8 = \underline{3} + \underline{5}$

$8 = \underline{5} + \underline{3}$

$8 - \underline{3} = \underline{5}$

$8 - \underline{5} = \underline{3}$

---

1 Complete the number bond.

Write two addition sentences.

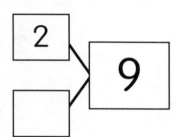

$\underline{} + \underline{} = 9$

$\underline{} + \underline{} = 9$

---

2 Complete the number bond.

Write two subtraction sentences.

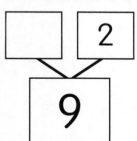

$9 - \underline{} = \underline{}$

$9 - \underline{} = \underline{}$

Number Partners for 8 and 9

3 Complete the number bond.
Write two subtraction sentences.

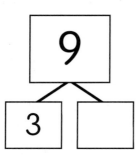

9

3 ▢

_____ = 9 − _____

9 − _____ = _____

4 Complete the number bond.
Write two addition sentences.

9

▢

5

9 = _____ + _____

_____ + _____ = 9

5 Complete the number bond.
Write four number sentences.

8

6 ▢

___ + ___ = 8   ___ − ___ = 2

8 = ___ + ___   ___ = 8 − ___

Jen has cards with numbers 1 to 9.

She adds two cards to get 10.

What are all the ways to make 10?

 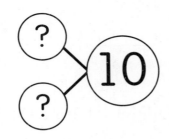

Model It **Find the ways to make 10.**

$1 + \_\_\_\_ = 10$ $\_\_\_\_ + 1 = 10$

$2 + \_\_\_\_ = 10$ $\_\_\_\_ + 2 = 10$

$3 + \_\_\_\_ = 10$ $\_\_\_\_ + 3 = 10$

$4 + \_\_\_\_ = 10$ $\_\_\_\_ + 4 = 10$

$5 + \_\_\_\_ = 10$

Number Partners for 10

10 beads. 6 are red. The rest are yellow.
How many are yellow? How do you know?

Model It Find $6 + \underline{\quad} = 10$. •

Start with 6.
Add counters to make 10.
How many did you add?

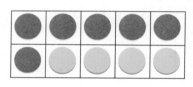 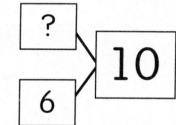

$6 + \underline{\quad} = 10$

Talk About It **Who is right? How do you know?** • • • • • • • • • • •

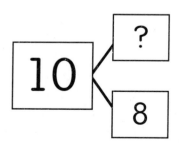

Buzz writes:

$10 + 8 = 2$

$2 + 10 = 12$

$8 = 10 - 2$

$6 = 8 - 2$

Boom writes:

$8 + 2 = 10$

$2 + 8 = 10$

$8 = 10 - 2$

$2 = 10 - 8$

Practice Together
Number Partners for 10

Write two number sentences.

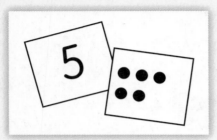

$$10 = \underline{\ 5\ } + \underline{\ 5\ }$$

$$10 - \underline{\ 5\ } = \underline{\ 5\ }$$

---

1 Complete the number bond.
Write two addition sentences.

[ ] [9]
[10]

$$10 = \underline{\ \ \ } + \underline{\ \ \ }$$

$$\underline{\ \ \ } + \underline{\ \ \ } = 10$$

---

2 Complete the number bond.
Write two subtraction sentences.

[ ] [9]
[10]

$$10 - 9 = \underline{\ \ \ }$$

$$9 = 10 - \underline{\ \ \ }$$

Number Partners for 10

3 Complete the number bond.
Write two subtraction sentences.

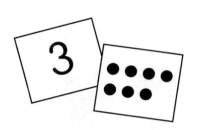

$$10 - \underline{\quad} = \underline{\quad}$$

$$10 - \underline{\quad} = \underline{\quad}$$

4 Complete the number bond.
Write two addition sentences.

$$10 = \underline{\quad} + \underline{\quad}$$

$$\underline{\quad} + \underline{\quad} = 10$$

5 Complete the number bond.
Write four number sentences.

$$\underline{\quad} + \underline{\quad} = 10 \qquad 10 - \underline{\quad} = \underline{\quad}$$

$$10 = \underline{\quad} + \underline{\quad} \qquad \underline{\quad} = 10 - \underline{\quad}$$

What does = mean?

= is the **equal sign**.

= means **is the same as**.

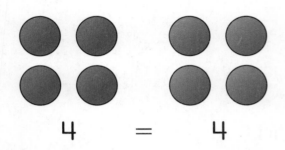

4 = 4

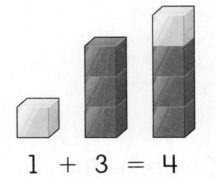

1 + 3 = 4

 **Think** **The total can go to the left or right of = .**

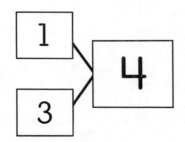

1 + 3 = ___

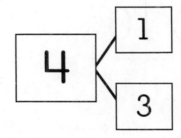

___ = 1 + 3

Talk About It

4 + 2 = 5   5 = 2 + 3

Are both number sentences true?

How do you know?

Explore Together
Understand the Equal Sign

Find partners that are equal.

Look at the → Use cubes. → Complete the
numbers.   Make partners.   number sentences.

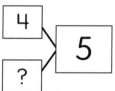

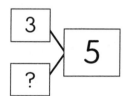

$4 + \underline{1} = 5$

$5 = 3 + \underline{2}$

$4 + \underline{1} = 3 + \underline{2}$

5 = 5

---

1   **Find partners that are equal.**

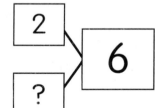

2 + ___ = 6   **6 = ___ + 3**

___ + ___ = ___ + ___

Talk About It •

Mia joins 2 cubes and 6 cubes.

Dan joins 4 cubes and 3 cubes.

Do they have the same number of cubes? How do you know?

Connect It
Understand the Equal Sign

2 **Draw** Is $3 + 5 = 5 + 3$ a true number sentence? Draw to explain why or why not.

3 **Evaluate** Circle the true number sentences.

$$4 = 6 \qquad\qquad 7 = 4 + 3$$

$$1 + 3 = 2 + 2 \qquad\qquad 4 + 2 = 1 + 6$$

$$2 + 7 = 5 + 3 \qquad\qquad 8 + 2 = 4 + 6$$

4 **Create** Make true number sentences.

$$\underline{} + \underline{} = 3 + 7 \qquad\qquad 4 + 5 = \underline{} + \underline{}$$

Understand the Equal Sign

5 **Think about the equal sign.**

A: Write the number of shapes below each group.

Write = in the box if it is a true number sentence.

Write X in the box if it is not a true number sentence.

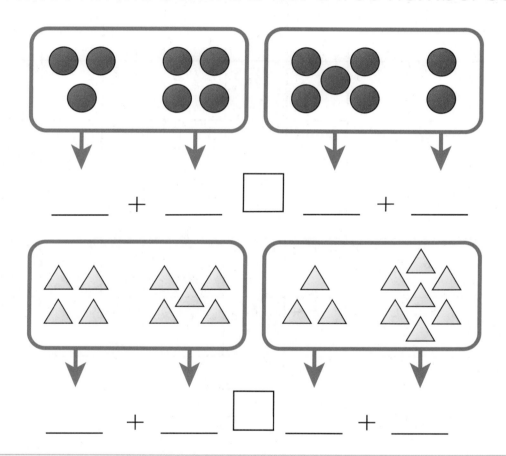

____ + ____ ☐ ____ + ____

____ + ____ ☐ ____ + ____

B: Use the number sentence that is not true.

Write a true number sentence. Show your work.

____ + ____ ☐ ____ + ____

Explore Together
Facts I Know

What addition facts do you know?

 **Model It** **Write the totals.** •••••••••••••••••••••••••••••••••••••

1 + 1	1 + 2	1 + 3	1 + 4	1 + 5	1 + 6	1 + 7	1 + 8	1 + 9
2 + 1	2 + 2	2 + 3	2 + 4	2 + 5	2 + 6	2 + 7	2 + 8	
3 + 1	3 + 2	3 + 3	3 + 4	3 + 5	3 + 6	3 + 7		
4 + 1	4 + 2	4 + 3	4 + 4	4 + 5	4 + 6			
5 + 1	5 + 2	5 + 3	5 + 4	5 + 5				
6 + 1	6 + 2	6 + 3	6 + 4					
7 + 1	7 + 2	7 + 3						
8 + 1	8 + 2							
9 + 1								

Learn Together
Facts I Know

What is the same about the facts in any row? What is different?

Model It Look at the facts in the colored boxes. • • • • • • • •

1 + 1 2	1 + 2 3	1 + 3 4	1 + 4 5	1 + 5 6	1 + 6 7	1 + 7 8	1 + 8 9	1 + 9 10
2 + 1 3	2 + 2 4	2 + 3 5	2 + 4 6	2 + 5 7	2 + 6 8	2 + 7 9	2 + 8 10	
3 + 1 4	3 + 2 5	3 + 3 6	3 + 4 7	3 + 5 8	3 + 6 9	3 + 7 10		
4 + 1 5	4 + 2 6	4 + 3 7	4 + 4 8	4 + 5 9	4 + 6 10			
5 + 1 6	5 + 2 7	5 + 3 8	5 + 4 9	5 + 5 10				
6 + 1 7	6 + 2 8	6 + 3 9	6 + 4 10					
7 + 1 8	7 + 2 9	7 + 3 10						
8 + 1 9	8 + 2 10							
9 + 1 10								

Talk About It •

How can the table help you learn addition facts?

Practice Together
Facts I Know

Fill in the blanks.

1

4 + ___ 7	___ + 4 8	4 + 5 ___	___ + ___ 10
___ + 3 8	5 + ___ 9	___ + ___ 10	

2

___ + 1 8	7 + ___ 9	___ + ___ 10
8 + ___ 9	___ + 2 10	

3

2 + ___ 6	___ + 5 7	2 + 6 ___	___ + 7 ___	2 + ___ 10
___ + 4 7	3 + ___ 8	___ + ___ 9	3 + ___ ___	

Practice by Myself
Facts I Know

 Fill in the table.

Partners of 7	Partners of 8	Partners of 9	Partners of 10
0 + 7 = ____	0 + 8 = ____		
1 + ____ = 7			
____ + 5 = 7			
3 + ____ = 7			
4 + ____ = 7			
____ + 2 = 7			
6 + ____ = 7			
____ + 0 = 7			

Unit 2 Review

Solve the problems.

1 Al has 5 toy trucks. He has 5 toy cars.
How many toy trucks and cars
does Al have?

5 + 5 = ____

2 There are 3 birds. More birds join them.
Now there are 7 birds.
How many birds join?

3 + ____ = 7

3 Make a true number
sentence.

____ + ____ = 2 + 7

4 **10 − 8 = ____**

5 **____ = 5 + 2**

6 Make a true number
sentence.

5 + ____ = 3 + 5

7 4 books and 2 books. How many books in all?

4 + 2 = _____   _____ = 2 + 4

Is 4 + 2 = 2 + 4 a true number sentence? _____
Draw to explain why or why not.

---

8 10 beads in all.

3 are red. The rest are yellow.
How many are yellow?

Complete the number bond.
Write four number sentences
for this problem.

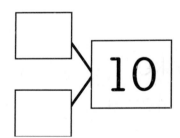

_____ + _____ = 10   10 − _____ = _____

10 = _____ + _____   _____ = 10 − _____

Put It Together

9 **Use the partners of 8 or 9.**

Write all the partners of 8 or 9 in the number bonds. Then write a true number sentence. Use two different partners. Explain how you know your number sentence is true.

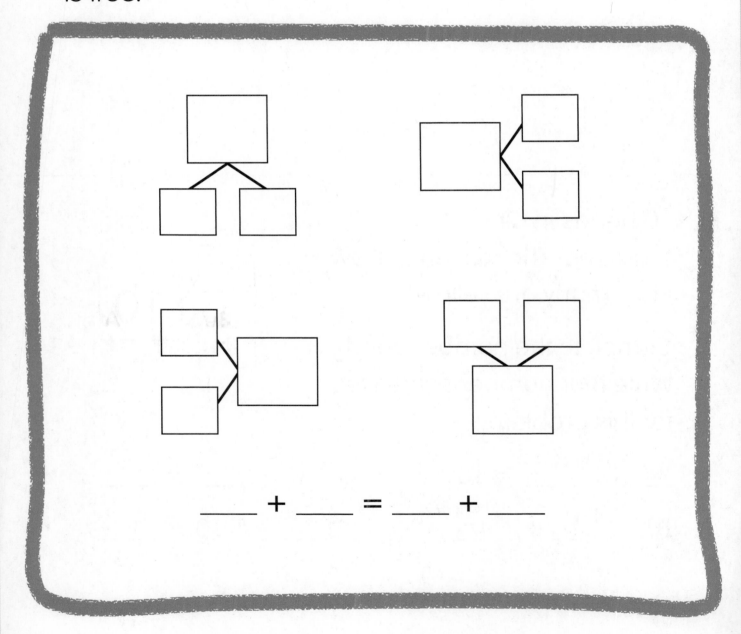

___ + ___ = ___ + ___

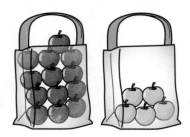

13 red apples and 5 green apples. Danna wants to give some apples to her aunt. She wants to keep some apples for herself. What math questions could Danna ask about the apples?

In this unit, you will learn ways to add and subtract to 20. Then you will be able to solve problems like Danna's.

✓ Self Check

Check off the skills you know now. Then see how many more you can check off after each lesson!

I can:	Before this unit	After this unit
name and write teen numbers.	☐	☐
make totals greater than 10.	☐	☐
make a ten to add.	☐	☐
add three numbers.	☐	☐
make a ten to subtract.	☐	☐
solve addition and subtraction word problems.	☐	☐

Understand
Teen Numbers

What are teen numbers?

Say the teen numbers. Circle the ones that end in *teen*.

Teen numbers: 11, 12, 13, 14, 15, 16, 17, 18, 19

 **A teen number is 1 ten plus some ones.** · · · · · · · · · ·

Circle the ten. Write the ones.

11   is   **10**   plus   _____ one

12   is   **10**   plus   _____ ones

 ·

Do 10 and 11 have the same number of tens?

The same number of ones?

Explore Together
Understand Teen Numbers

✋ **Show 13.**

Count the cubes. → Put the cubes in 10-frames. → Color and write the ones.

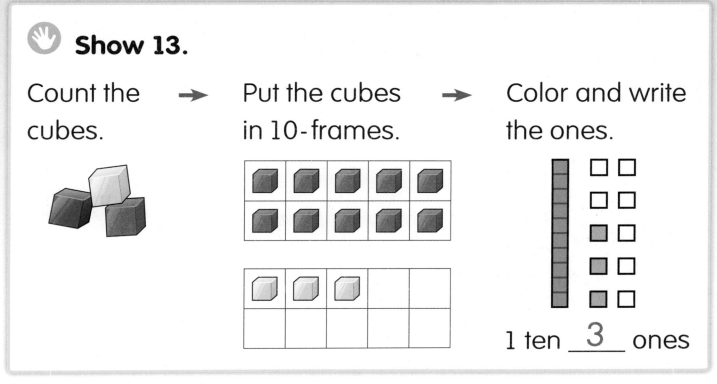

1 ten __3__ ones

① **Show 14.**

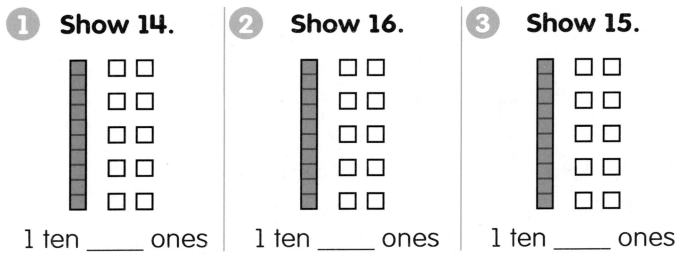

1 ten ____ ones

② **Show 16.**

1 ten ____ ones

③ **Show 15.**

1 ten ____ ones

💬 **Talk About It** •

What is the same about the numbers?
What is different?

Understand Teen Numbers

④ Compare Cora has 10 cubes and 7 more cubes.
Dan has 18 cubes. Who has more cubes?

⑤ Apply Complete each number bond.
Write number sentences.

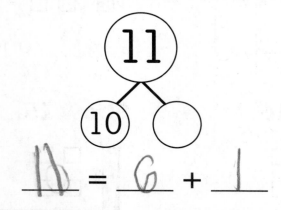

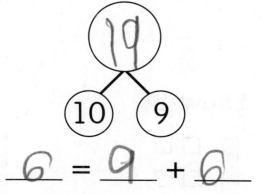

11 = 6 + 1   6 = 9 + 6

⑥ Explain Buzz says that this shows 4.
Do you agree? Why or why not?

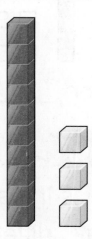

Show What I Know
Understand Teen Numbers

7 **Think about teen numbers.**

A: Draw more stickers.
Make two different teen numbers.

B: Make number bonds.
Then write your teen numbers.

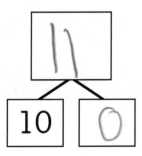

_____ is the same as

_____ ten _____ ones

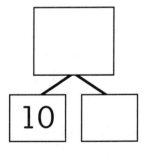

_____ is the same as

_____ ten _____ ones

How do you find partners of teen numbers?

You know that 12 is 10 + 2.

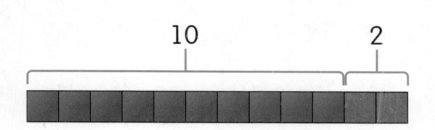

10   2

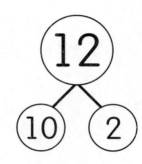

12

10   2

Think Change the first addend. Find the partner. ·········

12 = 10 + 2

12 = 9 + 3

12 = 8 + 4

12 = 7 + 5

12 = 6 + 12

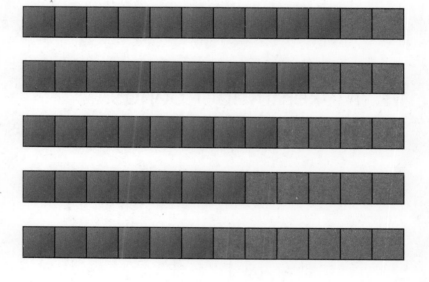

Talk About It ·····················

Change the order of the addends.

What happens when you add?

Understand Sums Greater than 10

 10 + ? = 13

Use cubes. ➡ Find the partner. ➡ Complete the number bond and number sentence.

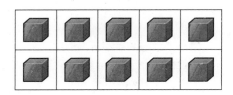

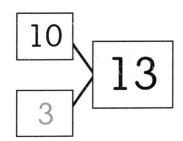

$10 + \underline{\ 3\ } = 13$

---

1 **9 + ? = 13**

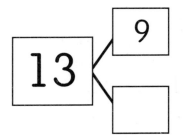

$9 + \underline{\quad} = 13$

2 **8 + ? = 13**

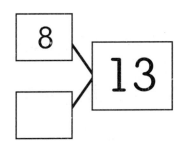

$8 + \underline{\quad} = 13$

3 **7 + ? = 13**

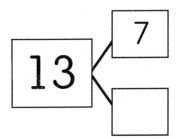

$7 + \underline{\quad} = 13$

 Talk About It •

How did you find the partners of 13?

Connect It
Understand Sums Greater than 10

4 **Interpret** Complete the number bond and number sentences.

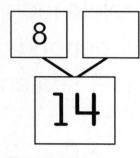

$14 = 8 + \underline{}$

$14 = \underline{} + 8$

5 **Illustrate** Use two colors. Color the circles. Then complete the number sentences.

$9 + \underline{} = 14$

$\underline{} + 9 = 14$

6 **Explain** Look at the model. Is Buzz correct? How do you know?

Buzz writes:

$9 + 5 = 15$

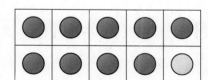 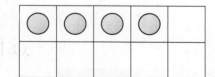

Understand Sums Greater than 10

7 **Think about different ways to make totals greater than 10.**

A: Draw to show partners of 15.
   Complete the number bonds.

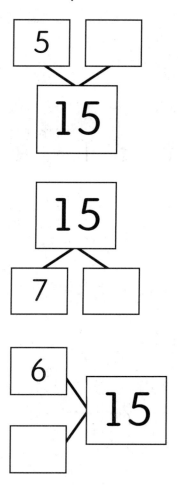

B: Show how to find the partners of 16.

---

8 children are on the bus. 5 more get on the bus.

How many are on the bus now?

$8 + 5 = ?$

Model It Find $8 + 5$. ••••••••••••••••••••••••••••••••

Start with 8. Take counters from 5 to **make a ten**.

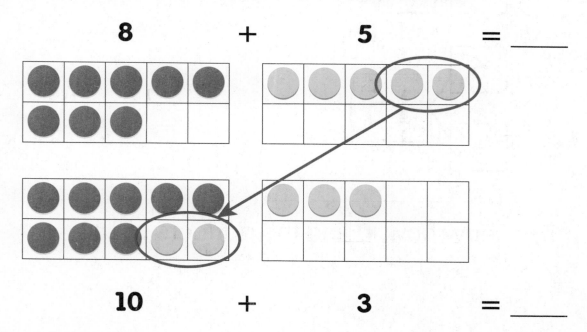

Learn Together
Make a Ten to Add

7 blocks are small. 5 blocks are big.

How many blocks are there in all?

How do you know?

7 + 5 = ?

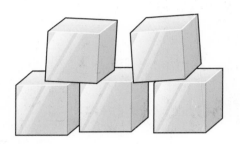

Model It **Find 7 + 5.**

Start with 7.

Add 3 to make 10.

Then add 2 more.

$$7 + 3 = 10 \qquad 10 + 2 = 12$$

$$7 + 5 = \underline{\quad\quad}$$

Talk About It **Do you agree? Why or why not?**

Boom says that 9 + 5 = 15.

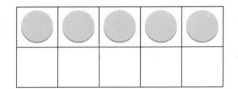

©Curriculum Associates, LLC   Copying is not permitted.

Practice Together
Make a Ten to Add

$8 + 6 = ?$

$8 + 2 = \underline{10}$

$10 + 4 = \underline{14}$

So, $8 + 6 = \underline{14}$

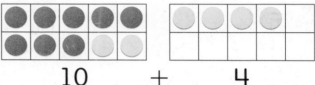

① $8 + 7 = ?$

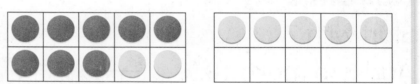

$8 + \underline{} = 10$

$10 + \underline{} = \underline{}$

$8 + 7 = \underline{}$

② $7 + 7 = ?$

| 6 | 7 | 8 | 9 | 10 | 11 | 12 | 13 | 14 | 15 |

$7 + \underline{} = 10$

$10 + \underline{} = \underline{}$

$7 + 7 = \underline{}$

Practice by Myself
Make a Ten to Add

3 7 + 6 = ?

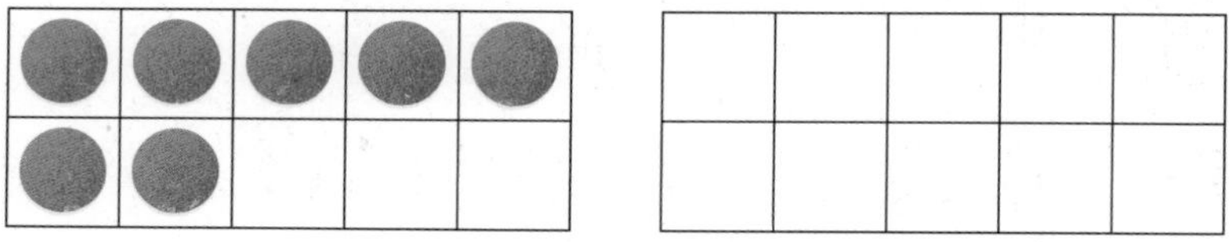

7 + ___ = ____

10 + ___ = ____

7 + 6 = ____

4 9 + 4 = ?

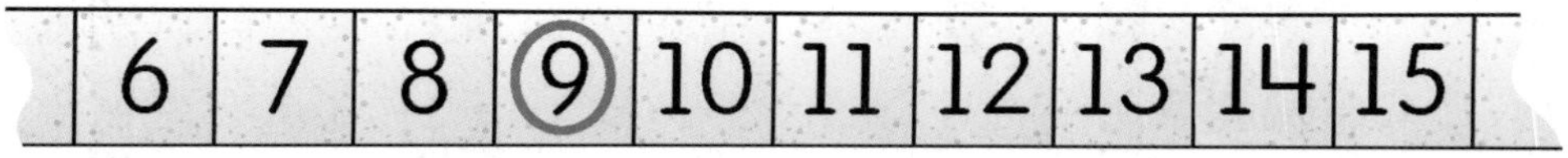

| 6 | 7 | 8 | ⑨ | 10 | 11 | 12 | 13 | 14 | 15 |

9 + 4 = ____

5 8 + 6 = ?

8 + 6 = ____

Pat collects 8 cans of food.

Max collects 2 cans. May collects 4 cans.

How many cans do they collect in all?

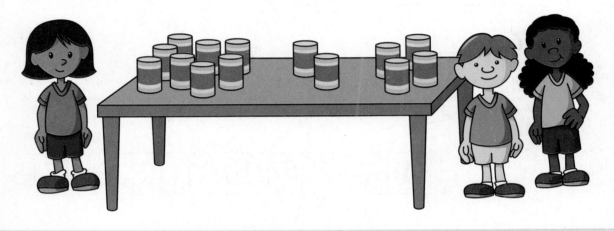

Model It Find 8 + 2 + 4. •

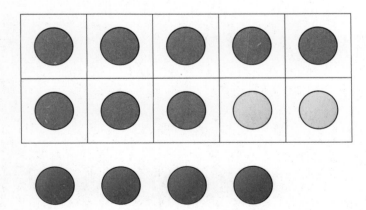

8 + 2 + 4

10 + 4 = 14

Learn Together
Make a Ten to Subtract

Coach has 14 hats. He gives out 6 hats.
How many hats are left?

Model It **Find 14 − 6. Think: 6 = 2 + 4.** ·······················

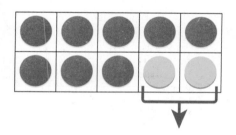

Take away 2.   Take away 4.

$14 - 4 =$ _10_

$10 - 2 =$ _8_

$14 - 6 =$ _8_

Talk About It **What is wrong?** ··························

Buzz finds 13 − 5.

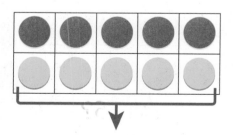   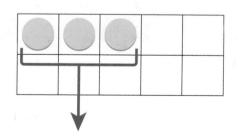

Take away 5.   Take away 3.

Practice Together
Make a Ten to Subtract

$16 - 7 = ?$

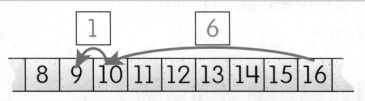

$16 - \underline{6} = \mathbf{10}$

$10 - \underline{1} = \underline{9}$

So, 16 − 7 = $\underline{9}$

1 $14 - 9 = ?$

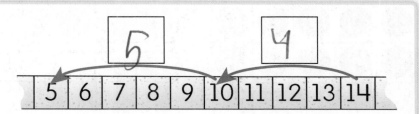

$14 - \underline{4} = \mathbf{10}$

$10 - \underline{6} = \underline{5}$

$14 - 9 = \underline{5}$

2 $17 - 8 = ?$

$17 - \underline{} = \mathbf{10}$

$10 - \underline{} = \underline{}$

$17 - 8 = \underline{}$

Make a Ten to Subtract

3 13 − 7 = ?

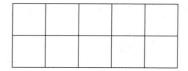

13 − 7 = ____

4 15 − 8 = ?

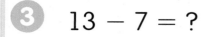

15 − 8 = ____

5 14 − 5 = ?

14 − 5 = ____

Solve the problems.

1 8 blocks are big. 7 blocks are small.
How many in all?

8 + ____ = ____

10 + ____ = ____

8 + 7 = ____

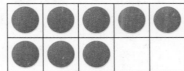

2 Max has 14 stickers. He gives away 5 stickers.
How many stickers are left?

14 − ____ = 10

10 − ____ = ____

14 − 5 = ____

| 6 | 7 | 8 | 9 | 10 | 11 | 12 | 13 | 14 | 15 |

3 4 green balls. 7 red balls. 3 blue balls. How many in all?

4 + 7 + 3 = ____

4 ____ = 13 − 6

5 16 is the same as

____ ten and ____ ones

6 17 = 10 + ____

17 = ____ + 8

7 6 children are on the bus.
5 more children get on.
4 children get on next.
How many children are
on the bus now?

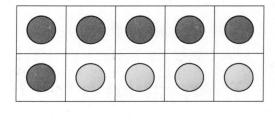

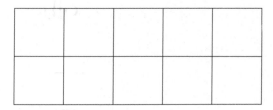

$$\overset{10}{\overbrace{6 + 5}} + 4 = \underline{\quad}$$

There are _____ children on the bus now.

---

8 Cam has 11 apples.
9 are red. The rest are green.
Complete the number bonds.
Then write two addition sentences.

_____ + 1 = 11

9 + _____ = 11

Cam has _____ green apples.

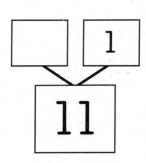

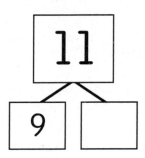

Put It Together

9 **Make a teen number.**

Then make a ten to subtract.

Draw more stickers to make 11, 12, 13, 14, or 15.
Then subtract 7 from your number.

____ – ____ = **10**

10 – ____ = ____

So, ____ – **7** = ____

 60 cherries and 50 grapes. The cherries and grapes are in bags of 10. Ben gives Emma some of the bags. What math questions could Ben ask about the bags of fruit?

In this unit, you will learn about tens and how to add and subtract tens. Then you will be able to solve problems like Ben's.

✓ Self Check

Check off the skills you know now. Then see how many more you can check off after each lesson!

I can:	Before this unit	After this unit
show numbers as tens.	☐	☐
count on a 120 chart.	☐	☐
find 10 more and 10 less than a number.	☐	☐
subtract 10 in my head.	☐	☐
add tens.	☐	☐
subtract tens.	☐	☐

Understand
Tens

What is a ten?

Ten is
10 ones.

Ten is the name for
a group of 10 ones.

Think   **What is 2 tens?** ·

2 **tens** is
___2___ groups of 10.

2 tens is
_20_ ones.

Talk About It ·

Look at the picture of 10 ones and the picture of 1 ten.
How are they the same?   Tkey

Understand Tens

 Show 20.

Count cubes. ➡ Make tens. ➡ Color. Write how many tens.

  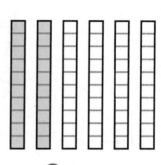

_2_ tens

1 **Show 30.**

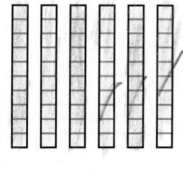

___ tens

2 **Show 40.**

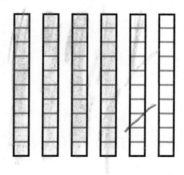

___ tens

3 **Show 50.**

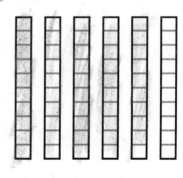

___ tens

 Talk About It •

Ana counts 3 tens. Micah counts 20 ones. Which is more?

Connect It
Understand Tens

4 **Draw** Show why 1 ten means the same as 10 ones.

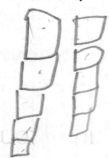

5 **Reason** Draw 1 ten and 10 more ones. How many tens in all?

6 **Explain** David says this shows 14. Do you agree? Why or why not?

It do not agree

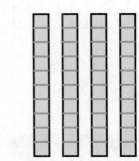

Understand Tens

7 **Think about making tens.**

A: Circle groups of 10.
Write how many.

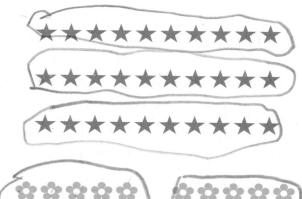

How many groups? 3

How many stars? 30

How many groups? 4

How many flowers? 40

How many groups? 5

How many stars? 05

B: Draw 21 beach balls.
Show how you know you have 21.

How does the 120 chart show numbers?

Model It Find numbers. •

Use blue. Color the numbers that have 2 ones.
Use red. Circle the numbers that have 3 tens.

1	2	3	4	5	6	7	8	9	10
11	12	13	14	15	16	17	18	19	20
21	22	23	24	25	26	27	28	29	30
31	32	33	34	35	36	37	38	39	40
41	42	43	44	45	46	47	48	49	50
51	52	53	54	55	56	57	58	59	60
61	62	63	64	65	66	67	68	69	70
71	72	73	74	75	76	77	78	79	80
81	82	83	84	85	86	87	88	89	90
91	92	93	94	95	96	97	98	99	100
101	102	103	104	105	106	107	108	109	110
111	112	113	114	115	116	117	118	119	120

Learn Together
The 120 Chart

How can you count on the 120 chart?

Model It • **Count up.** ••••••••••••••••••••••••••••••••••••

Count up 1 from 5. Then count up 1 from 18.

5 and 1 more is ____.

1	2	3	4	⑤	**6**	7	8	9	10
11	12	13	14	15	16	17	⑱	**19**	20

18 and 1 more is ____.

Count up 2 from 62. Then count up 2 from 75.

62 and 2 more is ____.

61	⑥②	63	**64**	65	66	67	68	69	70
71	72	73	74	⑦⑤	76	**77**	78	79	80

75 and 2 more is ____.

Count up 5 from 85. Then count up 5 from 90.

85 and 5 more is ____.

81	82	83	84	⑧⑤	86	87	88	89	⑨⓪
91	92	93	94	**95**	96	97	98	99	100

90 and 5 more is ____.

Talk About It **Who is right? How do you know?** •••••••••••

Boom says 70 and 5 more is 74.

Buzz says 70 and 5 more is 75.

Practice Together
The 120 Chart

Fill in the blanks. Use the chart.

31	32	33	34	35	36	37	38	39	40
41	42	43	44	45	46	47	48	49	50
51	52	53	54	55	56	57	58	59	60

1 **Start at 40.**   **Start at 55.**

1 more than 40 is _____.   1 more than 55 is _____.

2 more than 40 is _____.   2 more than 55 is _____.

5 more than 40 is _____.   5 more than 55 is _____.

2 **Count by 1:**   33, _____, 35, _____, 37, _____

Count by 2:   42, _____, _____, _____, 50

Count by 5:   40, 45, _____, _____, _____

Practice by Myself
The 120 Chart

Fill in the blanks. Use the chart.

91	92	93	94	95	96	97	98	99	100
101	102	103	104	105	106	107	108	109	110
111	112	113	114	115	116	117	118	119	120

3 **Start at 100.**   **Start at 115.**

1 more than 100 is _____.   1 more than 115 is _____.

2 more than 100 is _____.   2 more than 115 is _____.

5 more than 100 is _____.   5 more than 115 is _____.

4 **Count by 1:**   104, _____, 106, _____, 108, _____

Count by 2:   98, _____, _____, _____, 106

Count by 5:   95, 100, _____, _____, _____

Understand
10 More and 10 Less

What is 10 more and 10 less?

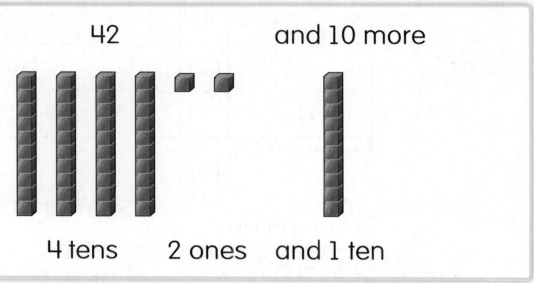

42   and 10 more

4 tens   2 ones   and 1 ten

Think   **10 more means adding 1 ten.** • • • • • • • • • • • • • • •

$$42 + 10 = 52$$

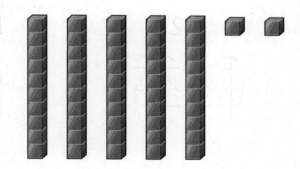

_____ tens   _____ ones

Talk About It •

How do the digits change when you add 10 to 42?

Understand 10 More and 10 Less

 Find 10 less than 37.

Use a 120 chart. → Color the → __27__ is 10
Color 37.   number   less than 37.
                     above 37.

21	22	23	24	25	26	27	28	29	30
31	32	33	34	35	36	37	38	39	40
41	42	43	44	45	46	47	48	49	50

1 **Find 10 more than 62.**
Color both numbers.

_____ is 10 more than 62.

2 **Find 10 less than 69.**
Color both numbers.

_____ is 10 less than 69.

51	52	53	54	55	56	57	58	59	60
61	62	63	64	65	66	67	68	69	70
71	72	73	74	75	76	77	78	79	80

Talk About It •

How does the 120 chart help you find 10 less
and 10 more? Why does this work?

Connect It
Understand 10 More and 10 Less

3 **Identify** What is 10 more than 96?

81	82	83	84	85	86	87	88	89	90
91	92	93	94	95	96	97	98	99	100
101	102	103	104	105	106	107	108	109	110

10 more than 96 is _____.

4 **Choose** Fill in the blanks. Use the numbers in the box.

_____ is 10 more than 58.

_____ is 10 less than 58.

_____ is 10 more than 88.

_____ is 10 less than 88.

78

48

68

98

5 **Explain** Buzz says 10 less than 84 is 83.
Do you agree? Why or why not?

Understand 10 More and 10 Less

6 **Think about 10 more and 10 less.**

A: Use digit cards to make numbers.

Write a number. Find 10 less and 10 more than your number.

☐ ☐

10 less than _____ is _____.

10 more than _____ is _____.

Write a different number. Find 10 less and 10 more than your number.

☐ ☐

10 less than _____ is _____.

10 more than _____ is _____.

B: Find 93 + 10. Tell how you know.

93 + 10 = _____

Tess has 30 erasers in a jar.
She gets 20 more.

How many erasers
does she have now?

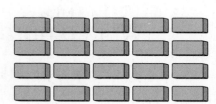

Model It **Find 30 + 20.**

Write the numbers as tens.
Then add the tens.

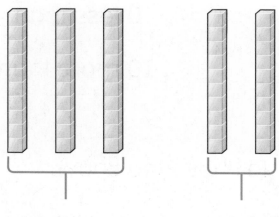

3 tens   +   2 tens = 5 tens

30 + 20 = _____

Learn Together
Add and Subtract Tens

Julie picks 70 berries.
Al picks 40 berries.

How many more
does Julie pick?

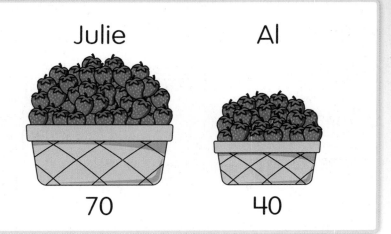

Julie   Al

70   40

Model It **Find 70 − 40.**

Use addition to subtract.
Write as tens.
Then add the tens.

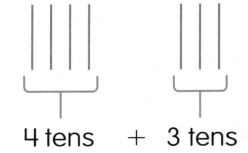

4 tens   +   3 tens

$40 + ? = 70$

4 tens + _____ tens = _____ tens

70 − 40 = _____

Talk About It **Who is right? How do you know?**

Buzz says 60 − 20 = 40.
Boom says 6 tens − 2 tens = 4 tens.

Practice Together
Add and Subtract Tens

50 gray birds.
30 red birds.

How many more gray birds?

50 − 30 = __20__

$30 + ? = 50$

| | | | |

3 tens   2 tens

---

1 10 blue flowers.
20 yellow flowers.

How many flowers in all?

10 + 20 = ___   **___ ten + ___ tens = ___ tens**

---

2 Find 90 − 40.

$4 + ? = 9$

4 tens + _____ tens = 9 tens

40 + ____ = 90   **90 − 40 = ____**

Add and Subtract Tens

3 60 paper clips.
50 are in a box.

How many are not
in the box?

$50 + ? = 60$

$|\ |\ |\ |\ |\quad|$

60 − 50 = ____

---

4 30 footballs and 30 basketballs.

What is the total number of balls?

30 + 30 = ____

____ tens + ____ tens = ____ tens

---

5 Find 80 − 20.

$2 + ? = 8$

2 tens + ____ tens = 8 tens

20 + ____ = 80　　　　　　　**80 − 20 = ____**

Unit 4 Review

Solve the problems.

1 35 ducks and 2 more ducks.

2 more than 35 is ____.

23	24	25	26	27	28
33	34	35	36	37	38
43	44	45	46	47	48

2 52 paper clips. 10 are in a box.
How many are not in the box?

41	42	43	44	45	46	47	48	49	50
51	52	53	54	55	56	57	58	59	60
61	62	63	64	65	66	67	68	69	70

52 − 10 = ____

3 **86 + 10 =** ____

4 ____ **= 80 − 10**

5 **Count by 1: 108,** ____ **, 110,** ____ **,** ____ **, 113**

6 The number of birds is the same as 6 tens.

Draw 6 tens.

6 tens is _____ groups of 10.   6 tens is _____ ones.

There are _____ birds.

---

7 Jo has 24 markers.

24 is _____ tens and _____ ones.

Bo has 10 more than Jo.   Mo has 10 fewer than Jo.

_____ = 24 + 10   24 − 10 = _____

Bo has _____ markers.   Mo has _____ markers.

8 Subtract tens.

Draw 5, 6, 7, 8, or 9 tens. Complete the problem using your number.

There are _____ shapes. 30 of them are squares. The rest are circles. How many are circles? Show your work.

_____ shapes are circles.

Jack has 27 cards. Kim has 34 cards. Owen has 20 cards. Jack wants to compare the numbers of cards. He wants to trade some cards. What math questions could Jack ask could about the cards?

In this unit, you will learn to compare numbers and to add two-digit numbers. Then you will be able to solve problems like Jack's!

✓ Self Check ••••••••••••••••••••••••••••••••••••••

Check off the skills you know now. Then see how many more you can check off after each lesson!

I can:	Before this unit	After this unit
rename numbers as tens and ones.	☐	☐
compare two-digit numbers.	☐	☐
add tens to any number.	☐	☐
add tens and ones.	☐	☐
regroup to add two-digit numbers.	☐	☐

What is a number as tens and ones?

You can show 32 as different tens and ones.

32 is 32 ones.

32 is 3 tens 2 ones.

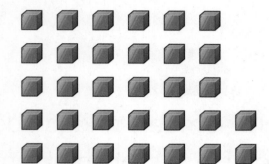

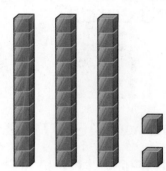

32 is 30 + 2.

Think There are other ways to show 32 as tens and ones.

32 is 2 tens 12 ones.

32 is 1 ten 22 ones.

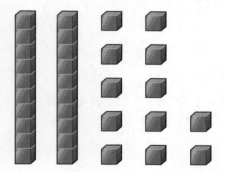

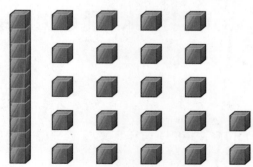

32 is 20 + _____.

32 is _____ + 22.

 Talk About It •

What are some ways to show 37 as tens and ones?

Understand Tens and Ones

 Show 23 as different tens and ones.
Use cubes.

Make 23 one way.   →   Make 23 another way.
Write the tens and ones.   Write the tens and ones.

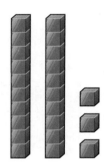

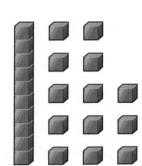

___2___ tens ___3___ ones   ___1___ ten ___13___ ones

1 **Show 45 as tens and ones two ways.**

_____ tens _____ ones

_____ tens _____ ones

2 **Show 54 as tens and ones two ways.**

_____ tens _____ ones

_____ tens _____ ones

 Talk About It •

What are other ways you can show these numbers?

Connect It
Understand Tens and Ones

3 **Draw** Show why 36 ones is the same as
3 tens 6 ones.

4 **Identify** Circle all the ways that show 76.

7 tens 6 ones   6 tens 7 ones

$60 + 7$ $70 + 6$

5 tens 26 ones   6 tens 16 ones

5 **Explain** Buzz says 5 tens 8 ones $= 5 + 80$.
Do you agree? Tell why or why not.

Understand Tens and Ones

6 **Think about how you can show numbers as different tens and ones.**

A: Circle some tens and ones.

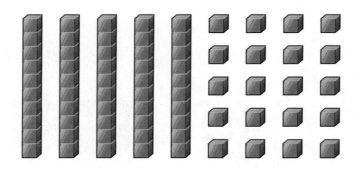

Write the number as tens and ones in two different ways. Write the two-digit number.

_____ tens _____ ones   _____ tens _____ ones   _____

B: Use the two digits from A. Write a different number. Show this number as tens and ones in two different ways.

Nora picks 52 apples. Nick picks 25 apples. Who picks more apples?

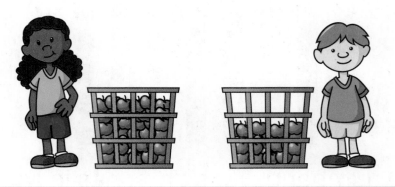

Model It Find 52 (?) 25. •

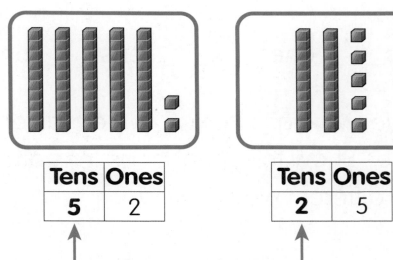

Tens	Ones
5	2

Tens	Ones
2	5

Compare tens.

5 tens **is greater than** 2 tens

5 tens > 2 tens

52 ◯ 25

Learn Together
Compare Numbers

Gabe collects 35 rocks.
Rose collects 39 rocks.
Who collects fewer rocks?

Model It Find 35 ? 39.

Compare tens.
Tens are the same.
Compare ones.

Tens	Ones
3	**5**

Tens	Ones
3	**9**

5 ones **is less than** 9 ones

5 ones < 9 ones

35 ◯ 39

5 ◯ 9

Talk About It Do you agree? Why or why not?

Fred collects 35 rocks.
Buzz says Fred collects more rocks than Gabe.

Part 2: Guided Instruction **103**

Practice Together
Compare Numbers

Jen has 48 coins. Kim has 14 coins.
Who has more coins?

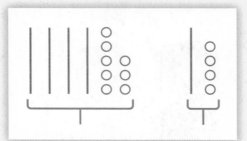

48   **14**

__4__ tens is greater than __1__ ten

48 ⊙ **14**

---

1 Fill in the blanks, then write <, >, or = in the circle.

____ tens ____ ones   ____ tens ____ ones

72 ◯ **72**

---

2 Write <, >, or = in the circle.

23 ◯ **27**

Practice by Myself
Compare Numbers

3 Fill in the blanks, then write <, >, or = in the circle.

____ tens ____ ones   ____ tens ____ ones

93 ◯ 48

4 Fill in the blanks, then write <, >, or = in the circle.

____ tens ____ ones   ____ tens ____ ones

16 ◯ 60

5 Write <, >, or = in the circle.

42 ◯ 45

29 ◯ 29

50 ◯ 36

Eli has 16 red fish
and 10 yellow fish.
How many fish in all?

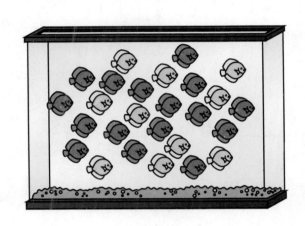

:: Model It **Find 16 + 10.** •

Add the tens.   Then add the ones.

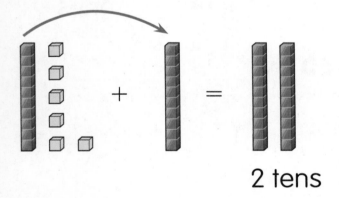

2 tens

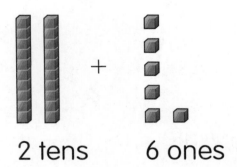

2 tens   6 ones

10 + 10 = _____   20 + 6 = _____

16 + 10 = _____

Add Tens to Any Number

50 blue balloons
and 13 red balloons.

How many balloons altogether?

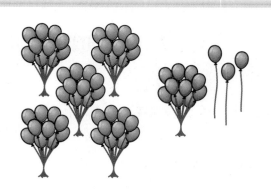

▦ Model It **Find 50 + 13.** •

Write the tens and ones.

50 + ┌─────┐
      │ 13 │
      └─────┘
       ╱   ╲
   ┌────┐ ┌───┐
   │ 10 │ │ 3 │
   └────┘ └───┘
 ⎯⎯⎯⎯⎯⎯⎯⎯⎯⎯⎯⎯
(50 + 10)+ 3 ⟶

Add the tens.
Then add the ones.

$50 + 10 = 60$

$60 + \underline{\quad} = \underline{\quad}$

$50 + 13 = \underline{\quad}$

💬 Talk About It **What is wrong?** •

20 baseballs and 12 footballs. How many balls?

What's wrong? $2 + 10 + 2 = 14$

▶ Show the right way. $\underline{\quad} + \underline{\quad} + \underline{\quad} = \underline{\quad}$

Practice Together
Add Tens to Any Number

10 blue marbles and 19 green marbles.
How many marbles in all?

$10 + 10 = \underline{20}$

$20 + 9 = \underline{29}$

$10 + 19 = \underline{29}$

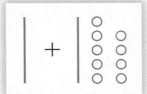

---

1   20 black cars and 32 white cars.
What is the total number of cars?

$20 + 32 = \underline{}$

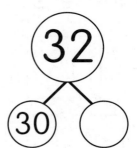

---

2   29 small ants and 10 big ants.
How many ants are there?

$\underline{} = 29 + 10$

Practice by Myself
Add Tens to Any Number

3 70 small paper clips
and 14 big paper clips.
How many paper clips?

_____ = 70 + 14

4 40 green frogs and 25 yellow frogs.
How many frogs?

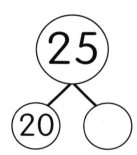

40 + 25 = _____

5 17 triangles and 20 squares.
How many shapes?

17 + 20 = _____

Add Tens and Add Ones

A necklace has 26 beads.
Another necklace has
32 beads.
How many beads altogether?

Model It Find 26 + 32.

Add the tens.

Then add the ones.

    2 tens 6 ones
+ 3 tens 2 ones
_____
    5 tens 8 ones = _____

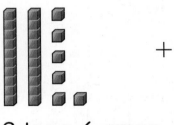 +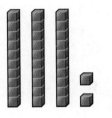

2 tens 6 ones   3 tens 2 ones

26 + 32 = _____

Learn Together
Add Tens and Add Ones

How many shells?

13 shells  14 shells

Model It **Find 13 + 14.** ·

Add the tens.
Then add the ones.

10 + 3
<u>10 + 4</u>
20 + 7 = ____

13 + 14 = ____

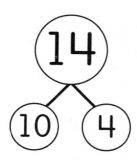

Talk About It **Who is right? How do you know?** · · · · · · · · ·

Boom: 2 tens 5 ones
<u>+ 1 ten   3 ones</u>
        3 tens 8 ones

Buzz: 20 + 5
<u>10 + 3</u>
30 + 8

Practice Together
Add Tens and Add Ones

34 big beads and 55 small beads.
How many beads?

30 + 4
50 + 5

$\boxed{80}$ + $\boxed{9}$ = $\boxed{89}$

34 + 55 = __89__

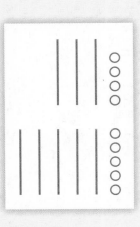

---

1 47 brown cows and
12 black cows.
How many cows in all?

47 + 12 = _____

40 + $\boxed{}$

$\boxed{}$ + **2**

$\boxed{}$ + $\boxed{}$ = $\boxed{}$

---

2 17 green pencils and
21 yellow pencils.
How many pencils?

_____ = 17 + 21

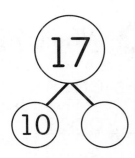

Practice by Myself
Add Tens and Add Ones

3   52 oak trees
and 35 pine trees.
How many trees in all?

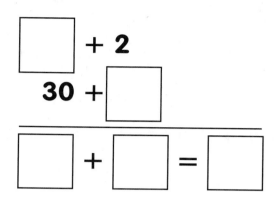

52 + 35 = ____

---

4   Manny has 43 cards.
Mark has 17 cards.
What is the total
number of cards?

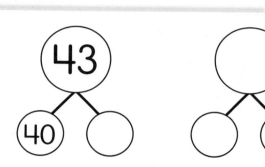

43 + 17 = ____

---

5   31 green grapes and 23 red grapes.
How many grapes altogether?

31 + 23 = ____

Lou has some erasers.
18 are blue. 7 are red.
How many erasers in all?

Model It   **Find 18 + 7.** •

Make the next ten.

18   +   7

Then add the tens and ones.

18 + 2   +   5

20 + 5 = _____

20 + 5

18 + 7 = _____

Learn Together
Add and Regroup

How many marbles?

35 marbles   27 marbles

Model It Find 35 + 27. ●

Add the tens and ones.

$$5 \text{ tens} \qquad 12 \text{ ones}$$
$$50 \quad + \quad 12$$
$$50 \quad + \quad 10 + 2 = \underline{\quad}$$

35 + 27 = _____

Talk About It Who is right? How do you know? ● ● ● ● ● ● ● ● ●

Buzz: 25 + 16 = 41   Boom: 25 + 16 = 31

Practice Together
Add and Regroup

27 flower stickers. 64 star stickers.
How many stickers?

    2 tens 7 ones
+ 6 tens 4 ones
    8 tens 11 ones = 80   +   11

                    80   + 10 + 1

27 + 64 = _91_

1 38 soccer balls and 46 kickballs.
How many balls?

_____ **= 38 + 46**

2 17 yellow flowers and 28 white flowers.
How many flowers altogether?

                        1 ten   7 ones
                    + 2 tens 8 ones

17 + 28 = _____

                    _____ tens _____ ones

Add and Regroup

3 33 math books and 27 reading books.
What is the total number of books?

33 + 27 = ____

4 48 circles and 35 squares.
How many shapes?

____ = 48 + 35

4 tens 8 ones
+ 3 tens 5 ones
_____

____ tens ____ ones

5 17 gold stars and 29 silver stars.
How many stars in all?

17 + 29 = ____

Solve the problems.

1. Ali picks 73 pears.
   Greg picks 37 pears.
   Who picks more pears?

   73 ◯ 37

   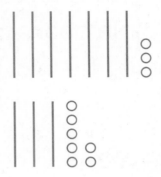

   _____ picks more pears.

2. 25 pink shells.
   34 brown shells.
   How many shells in all?

   25 + 34 = ____

   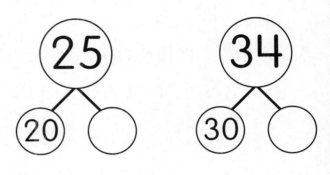

3. Circle ways to show 38.

   3 tens 8 ones   30 + 8

   80 + 3   2 tens 18 ones

4. 20 + 51 = ____

5. Write <, >, or = in the circle.

   54 ◯ 56   19 ◯ 19

6. ____ = 45 + 23

7 42 red birds. 46 blue birds.

Are there fewer red birds or blue birds?

Write the tens and ones.

Then write <, >, or = in the circle.

Tens	Ones

Tens	Ones

42 $\bigcirc$ 46

There are _____ red birds than blue birds.

---

8 27 circles and 29 triangles.

How many shapes in all?

    2 tens 7 ones
  + 2 tens 9 ones

_____ tens _____ ones

_____ = 27 + 29

There are _____ shapes in all.

Put It Together

9 **Add two numbers.**

Use the digits 5 and 7 to write a number.
Add your number to 28.
Show your work.

Shapes

Eve has some shapes. She wants to put shapes together to make a new shape. She wants to make equal parts. What math questions could Eve ask about the shapes?

In this unit, you will learn about shapes and about equal parts of shapes. Then you will be able to solve problems like Eve's.

✓ **Self Check** ....

Check off the skills you know now. Then see how many more you can check off after each lesson!

I can:	Before this unit	After this unit
use sides and corners to name shapes.	☐	☐
put shapes together to make new shapes.	☐	☐
break shapes into halves.	☐	☐
break shapes into fourths.	☐	☐

Understand
Shapes

How do you know the names of shapes?

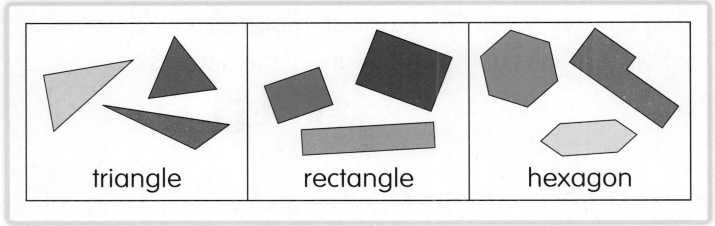

| triangle | rectangle | hexagon |

Think You look at the sides and corners. · · · · · · · · · · · · · · ·

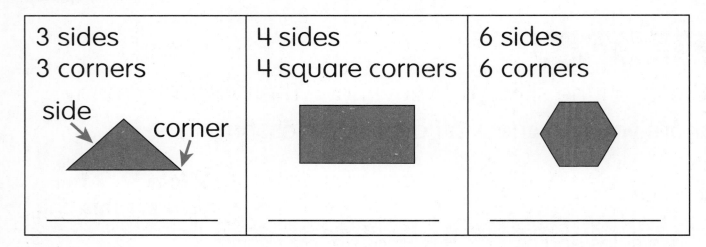

3 sides
3 corners

side   corner

4 sides
4 square corners

6 sides
6 corners

Talk About It ·

How are triangles, rectangles, and hexagons alike?

How are they different?

Understand Shapes

 Sort shapes with 4 sides and 4 corners.

Make a dot •
if true.
Make an **X**
if not true.

→ Describe these rectangles.

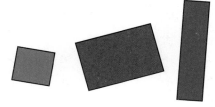

X 4 sides the same length

• 4 square corners

• opposite sides the same length

---

1 **Describe these squares.**

__ 4 sides the same length

__ 4 square corners

__ opposite sides the
same length

2 **Describe these
rhombuses.**

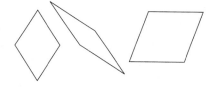

__ 4 sides the same length

__ 4 square corners

__ opposite sides the
same length

💬 **Talk About It** •

How are these shapes alike? How are they different?

Connect It
Understand Shapes

3 **Classify** Color the shapes.

triangles ▪ hexagons ▪ rectangles ▪ rhombuses ▪

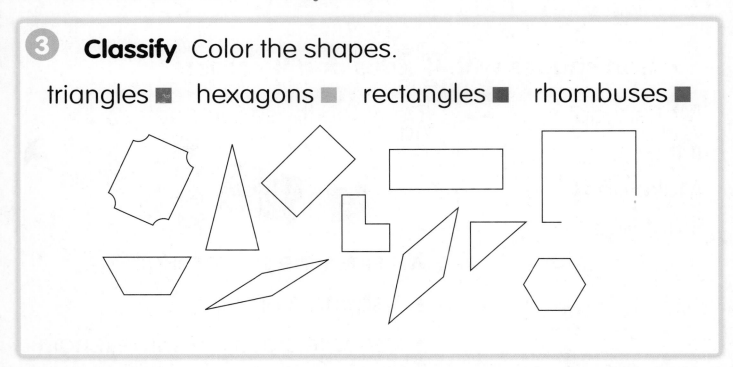

4 **Create** Draw the shape named in each box.

rhombus	trapezoid	square

5 **Evaluate** Eve says this shape is a rectangle.
Do you agree?
Why or why not?

Understand Shapes

6 **Make the same shape in different ways.**

A: Choose a shape to draw. Circle its name.

hexagon   triangle   rectangle
rhombus   square   trapezoid

Draw 3 of your shapes. Make each one different in some way.

B: How are your shapes different? How are they alike?

Understand
Putting Shapes Together

How can you put shapes together?

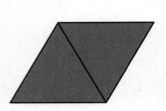  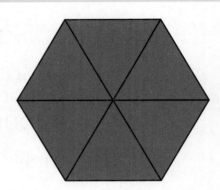

2 triangles make a rhombus

1 rhombus and 1 triangle make a trapezoid

6 triangles make a hexagon

 Think **You can make the same shape in different ways.**

Show other ways to put together shapes to make a hexagon.

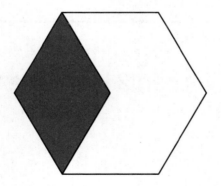 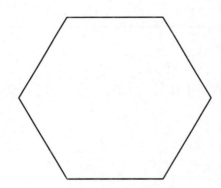

 Talk About It

How did you put together shapes to make a hexagon?

Understand Putting Shapes Together

 Put together shapes to make new shapes.

Use shapes. → Put shapes together. Trace each shape. → Make a new shape. Trace each shape.

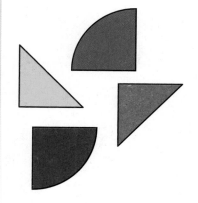

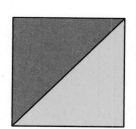

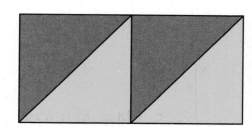

1 **Make this.**

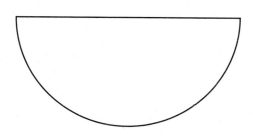

2 **Then make this.**

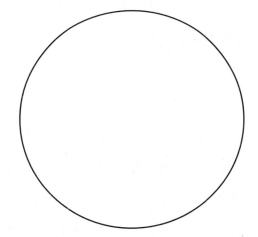

 Talk About It •

What other shapes can you make with shape pieces?

Connect It
Understand Putting Shapes Together

3 **Analyze** Color to show how to make this rectangle.

Use 2 shapes.   Use 3 shapes.

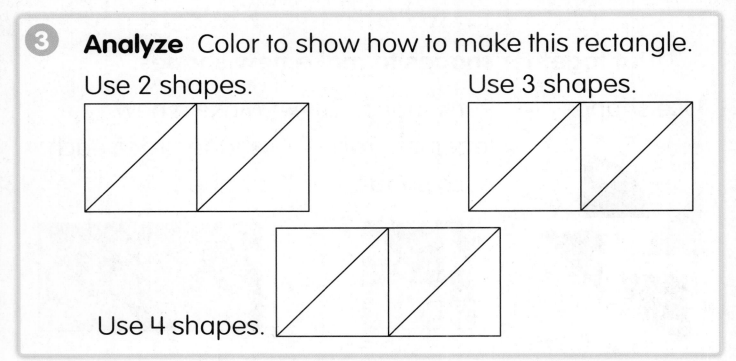

Use 4 shapes.

4 **Create** Use the shapes
from Problem 3 to
make a trapezoid.
Draw it.

5 **Evaluate** Buzz says the 2 triangles make a square.
Boom says the shape is not a square.
Who is right? How do you know?

Understand Putting Shapes Together

6 **Think about how to put shapes together.**

A: Use 4 or more shapes to make 2 new shapes. Draw them.

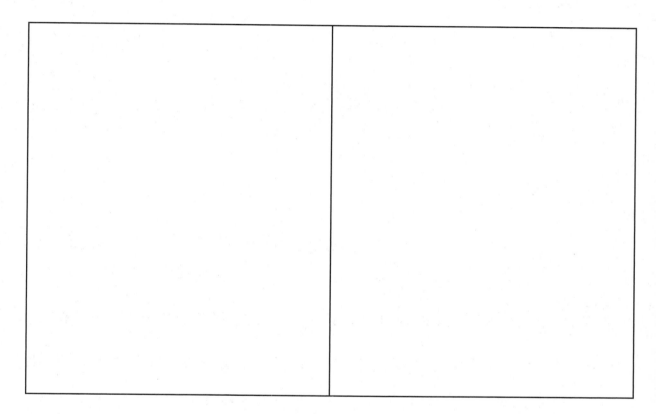

B: Circle one shape above. Write how many of each shape you used.

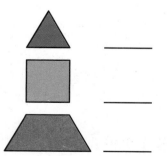 _____

_____

_____

 _____

_____

Understand
Breaking Shapes into Parts

How can you break shapes into equal parts?

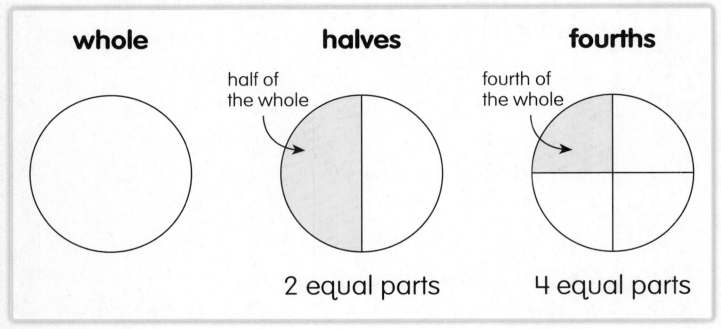

whole

halves

half of the whole

fourths

fourth of the whole

2 equal parts

4 equal parts

 **Think** **Equal parts cover an equal amount of the shape.**

Draw another way to fold the square into equal parts.

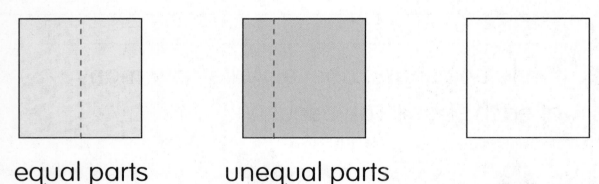

equal parts   unequal parts

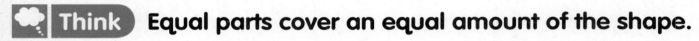 **Talk About It** •

How can you find out if two parts are equal?

Understand Breaking Shapes into Parts

 Fold shapes into equal parts.

Fold each shape. → Draw equal parts. → Circle the word that describes the parts.

 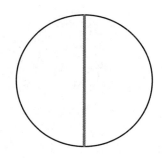 

halves

fourths

---

1 **Draw 4 equal parts.**

halves

fourths

2 **Draw 4 equal parts.**

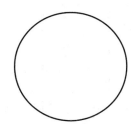

halves

quarters

 Talk About It •

Look at a half of a circle. Look at a fourth of a circle.

Which part is larger?

Connect It
Understand Breaking Shapes into Parts

3 **Explain** Jake's pizza is cut into 2 equal pieces. Kim's pizza is cut into 4 equal pieces. Which pieces are smaller? Show how you know.

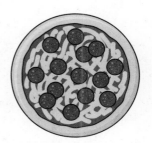 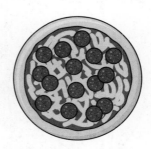

Jake's pizza   Kim's pizza

4 **Identify** Write how many equal parts.

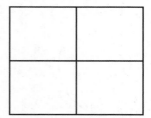

_____ equal parts

5 **Analyze** Buzz says that he shaded a quarter of this shape. Do you agree? Why or why not?

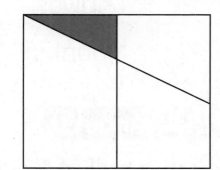

Understand Breaking Shapes into Parts

6 **Think about breaking shapes into equal parts.**

A: Ben has these cookies.

He shares the cookies with a friend.

They each get equal parts.

Color what Ben gets.

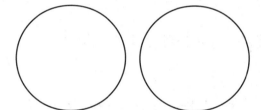  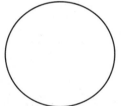 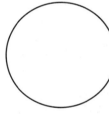

B: 4 friends share the cookies.

Color what Ben gets.

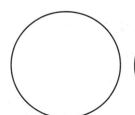 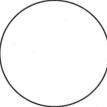 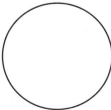 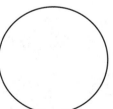 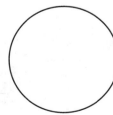

Unit 6 Review

Solve the problems.

1 How many equal parts are there?

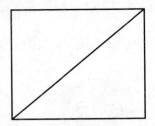

____ equal parts

---

2 This circle shows

_____.

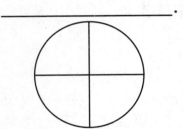

This circle shows

_____.

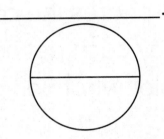

Which circle has larger parts? Color it.

---

3 Draw a trapezoid.

4 How many triangles?

____

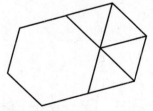

---

5 Circle the rectangle.

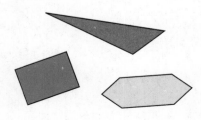

6 Break the shape into 1 and 1 .

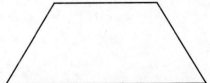

7 What shape is this? _____

Put two of these shapes together. Draw.
What shape do they make?

The two _____ make a _____.

---

8 Circle the words that describe a rhombus.

3 sides

4 sides the same length

1 square corner

opposite sides the same length

6 sides

Put It Together

9 **Make shapes.**

Put together 2 or 4 triangles like this ◣.

Make a shape with 4 sides. Describe the shape.

The shape is a _____.

It has _____ equal parts.

Circle the word that describes
the equal parts.

halves   fourths.

Use the shape you made.
Add some other shapes
to make a new shape.

Draw the new shape.

How Many? How Much? How Long?

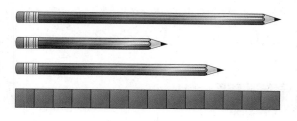

Sara has pencils of different lengths. She wants to know the length of the pencils. What math questions could Sara ask about the pencils?

In this unit, you will learn how to sort objects, tell time, and measure length. Then you will be able to solve problems like Sara's.

✓ Self Check

Check off the skills you know now. Then see how many more you can check off after each lesson!

I can:	Before this unit	After this unit
sort and count objects.	☐	☐
compare data.	☐	☐
order objects by length.	☐	☐
compare lengths of objects.	☐	☐
measure lengths of objects.	☐	☐
tell time to the hour and half-hour.	☐	☐

What shapes are there? How many of each shape?

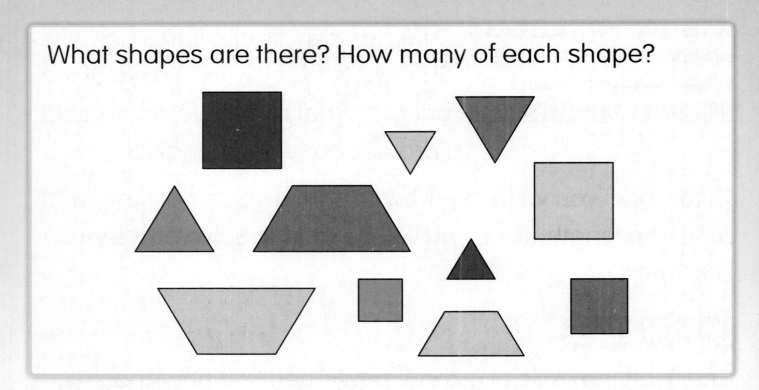

Model It   Make a chart.

Sort by shape. You can make a tally chart to count.

You can also make a chart with numbers.

Shapes	How Many
△	‖‖‖
□	
⏢	

Shapes	How Many
△	
□	
⏢	

Learn Together
Sort and Count

What color are the pencils?

How many of each color?

 Model It Make a picture graph. ● ● ● ● ● ● ● ● ● ● ● ● ● ● ● ● ● ● ●

Sort and count.

Pencils	How Many
✏	||||
✏	
✏	

Use circles to show how many.

Pencils	How Many
✏	O O O O
✏	
✏	

 Talk About It Do you agree? Why or why not? ● ● ● ● ● ● ● ● ● ● ●

Buzz says he can sort the pencils by size.

Practice Together
Sort and Count

How many of each kind of ball are there?

You can make a tally chart.
You can make a picture graph.

1 Complete the tally chart.

Ball	How Many
🏈	|||
⚫	
⚽	

2 Complete the picture graph.

Ball	How Many
🏈	O O O
⚫	
⚽	

Practice by Myself
Sort and Count

Use the data.

Favorite Fruit

3 Make a tally chart.

Favorite Fruit	How Many
🍎	
🍌	
🍐	

Make a chart with numbers.

Favorite Fruit	How Many
🍎	
🍌	
🍐	

4 Make a picture graph.

Favorite Fruit	How Many
🍎	
🍌	
🍐	

Compare Data

Children name their pets. They make a picture graph with the data. How many have dogs or cats?

Our Pets

Bird	😊 😊
Dog	😊 😊 😊 😊 😊 😊 😊
Cat	😊 😊 😊 😊

Model It **Find how many children have dogs or cats.**

Each picture shows 1 child. Count the pictures for dogs. Count the pictures for cats. Then add.

Our Pets

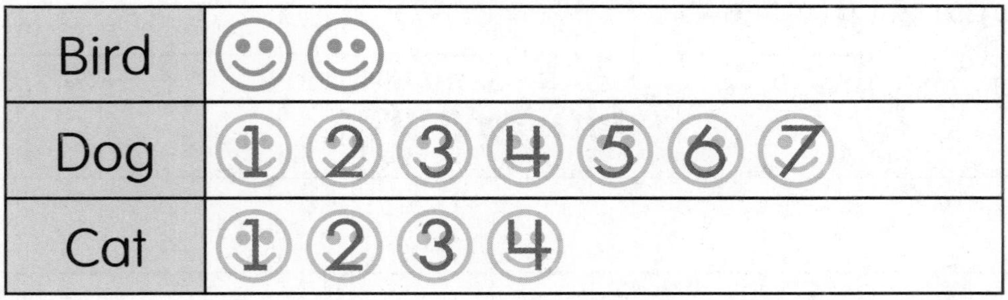

Bird	😊 😊	
Dog	① ② ③ ④ ⑤ ⑥ ⑦	_____ dogs
Cat	① ② ③ ④	_____ cats

$7 + 4 =$ _____

_____ **children have dogs or cats.**

Compare Data

How many more 🍐 than 🍎 ?

Favorite Fruits	How Many
🍐	14
🍌	8
🍎	12

▦ Model It

Color the squares to show how many.

14 is how many more than 12?

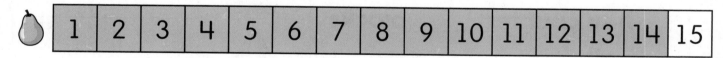

There are ____ more 🍐 than 🍎 .

💬 Talk About It

Look at the chart. What other questions can you ask?
What answers can you find?

Practice Together
Compare Data

Circle the fruit that the most children like.

Fruit	Number of Children
🍎	☺ ☺ ☺ ☺ ☺ ☺
🍓	☺ ☺ ☺ ☺ ☺
(🍇)	☺ ☺ ☺ ☺ ☺ ☺ ☺ ☺

1 Children counted their blocks. How many blocks did they count in all?

They counted _____ blocks in all.

Blocks	How Many
◆	9
▽	4
△	6

2 The tally chart shows Ms. Lee's markers.

Marker	Tally Marks
Blue	ⵣⵣ ⵣⵣ II
Red	ⵣⵣ III
Yellow	ⵣⵣ ⵣⵣ ⵣⵣ

How many more yellow than red? _____

How many fewer red than blue? _____

Practice by Myself
Compare Data

3 The tally chart shows what children like best.
Write the number for each object.
Circle the one that the most children like.

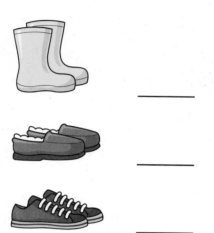

_____

_____

_____

Object	Tally Marks
	卌 卌 II
	卌 III
	卌 卌 卌 III

4 Circle what more children like.
Write how many more.

 or _____ **more**

Circle what fewer children like.
Write how many fewer.

 or _____ **fewer**

Three dogs with collars.

Which collar is the longest?

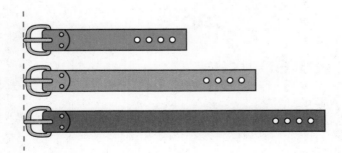 **Model It** **Compare lengths.** ·

Lay the collars on a table.

Line up one end.

Put them in order from shortest to longest.

The _____ **collar is the longest.**

The _____ **collar is the shortest.**

Learn Together
Order Objects by Length

Ron puts books on a shelf.
He wants to order them
from shortest to tallest.
Which book is shortest?

Model It **Order the books from tallest to shortest.**

Stand the books on a shelf.
Circle the shortest.
Put an X on the tallest.

Talk About It **Do you agree? Why or why not?**

Boom says the red flower is the shortest.

Practice Together
Order Objects by Length

Color the worm that is the shortest.
The middle worm is longest.
The top worm is shorter than
the bottom worm.

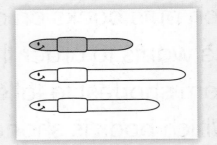

1 Draw lines to show
which pencil is longest
and which is shortest.

shortest 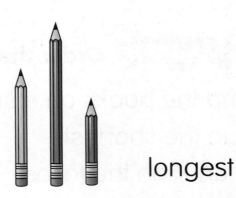 longest

2 Read the clues.
Then color the dogs.

The red dog is longest.

The blue dog is shorter
than the yellow dog.

Practice by Myself
Order Objects by Length

3 Read the clues.
Then color the bats.

The green bat is shortest.
The red bat is longer than
the blue bat.

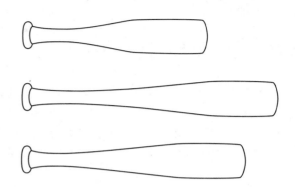

4 Circle the word that makes the
sentence true.

The green balloon is shorter / longer
than the orange balloon.

5 Draw a line that is taller than both rectangles.

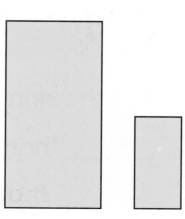

Compare Lengths

Which table is longer?

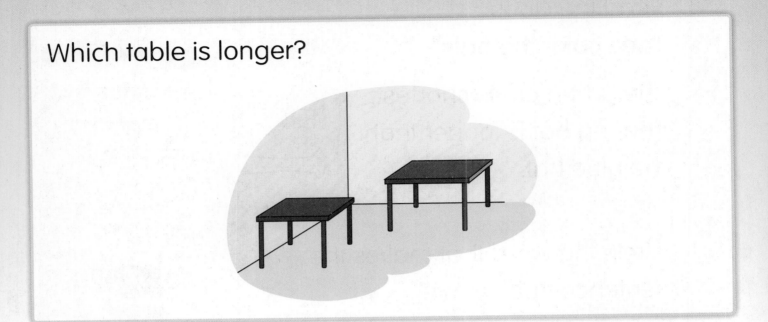

![Model It] **Compare lengths.** •

Use a piece of string. Compare it to the length
of each table.

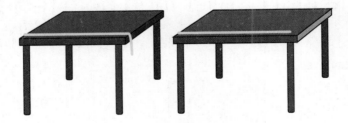

The gray table is longer than the string.

The brown table is _____ than the string.

So the gray table is _____ than the brown table.

Learn Together
Compare Lengths

Which object is shorter?

Model It Use a paper strip. •

Compare each object to the paper. Write shorter or longer.

_____   _____

The shoe is _____ than the spoon.

Talk About It Do you agree? Why or why not? • • • • • • • • • •

Chris is shorter than Amy.

Ray is taller than Amy.

Boom says Chris is taller than Ray.

Practice Together
Compare Lengths

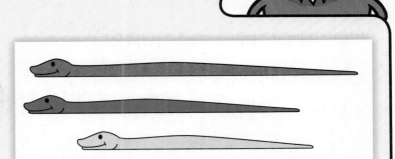

The red snake is longer than the blue snake.

The blue snake is longer than the yellow snake.

The _____red_____ snake is the longest.

1 Draw a line that is shorter than the triangle.
Circle the tallest object.

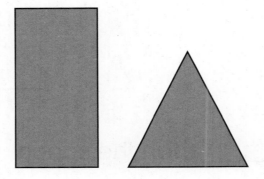

2 The crayon is shorter than the pencil.
The pencil is shorter than the notebook.

The crayon is _____ than the notebook.

Compare Lengths

3 Compare lengths.
Then circle the correct words.

is (longer than, shorter than) .

4 Draw a line that is taller than the star.
Which of the three pictures is tallest? Circle it.

5 The bee is longer than the ant.
The worm is longer than the bee.

The ant is _____ than the worm.

Length Measurement

How do you measure length?

Length tells you how long an object is.

You can find the length of a pencil.

Length

Think **You can use tiles to measure length.**

Line up the edge of the first tile with the edge of the pencil.

Count the tiles.

There are 10 tiles.

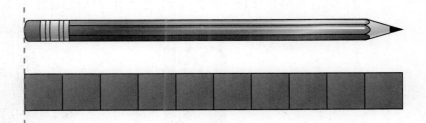

The pencil is _____ tiles long.

 Talk About It

Do the tiles need to be the same size?
Why or why not?

Understand Length Measurement

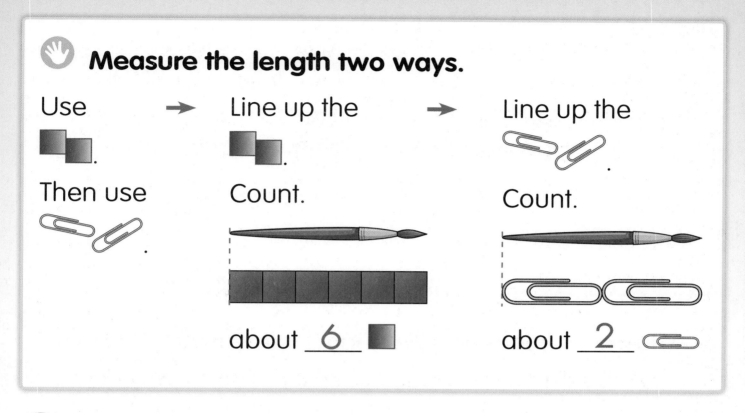

✋ **Measure the length two ways.**

Use ➡️ Line up the ➡️ Line up the

Then use

Count.

Count.

about __6__ 🟥

about __2__ 🔗

---

1 **Measure the length two ways.**

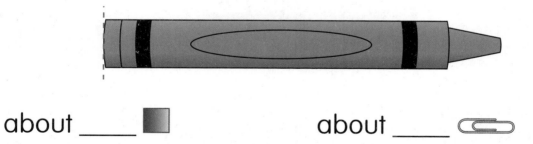

about ____ 🟥   about ____ 🔗

💬 **Talk About It** •

Do you need more 🟥 or 🔗 to measure the crayon?
Why?

Connect It
Understand Length Measurement

2 **Explain** Buzz says this string is 8  long. Boom says that is wrong. How does Boom know?

3 **Reason** Boom uses 8 squares to measure a ribbon. Did Boom measure the right way? Why or why not?

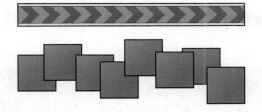

4 **Analyze** Boom says that his leaf is 4 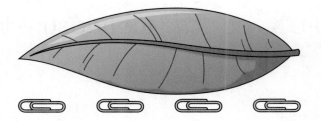 long. Do you agree? Why or why not?

Show What I Know
Understand Length Measurement

5 **Think about measuring length.**

A: Use 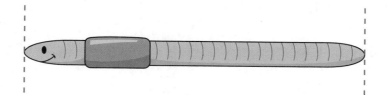 and ▬ . Circle the correct answer.

Does it take more ▪ or more ▬ to measure the worm?

Does it take fewer ▪ or fewer ▬ to measure the ladybug?

B: Draw a pencil. Measure it with ▪ and ▬ .

about _____ ▪   about _____ ▬

It is 2 o'clock.

Next, it is just past 2 o'clock.

Then it is almost 3 o'clock.

Where is the **hour hand** at each time?

hour

Model It   **Show the hour hand.** •

Draw the **hour hand** to show the time.

2 o'clock   just past 2 o'clock   almost 3 o'clock

Learn Together
Tell Time

What time do these clocks show?

▦ Model It **Read the time.** •

The **minute hand** is halfway around the clock.
The hour hand is halfway between 9 and 10.

It is half past ____.

It is 30 minutes after ____.

It is ____:30,
or nine thirty.

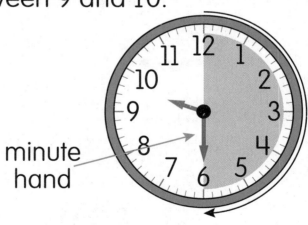

minute
hand

💬 Talk About It **Do you agree? Why or why not?** • • • • • • • • • • •

Buzz says 9:30 is halfway between 9:00 and 10:00.
So, 30 minutes is the same as a half hour.

Practice Together
Tell Time

These clocks show the same time.

What time is it?

It is __7__ o'clock.

---

1 Circle the clock that shows 4:00.

---

2 It is half past 3. Draw the time on these clocks.

 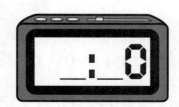

Lesson 34

Practice by Myself
Tell Time

3 Read the digital clock. Draw the hands to show the time.

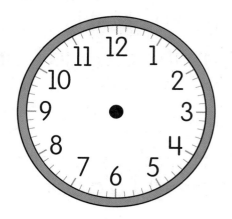

4 Circle the clock that shows 11:00.

5 It is eight thirty. Draw the times on these clocks.

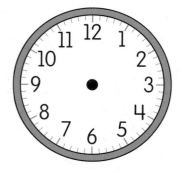

Unit 7 Review

Solve the problems.

1 The blue belt is _____ than the orange belt.

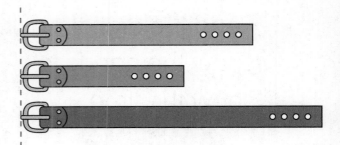

2 It is eight o'clock. Show the time on these clocks.

 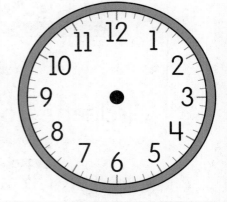

3 Make a tally chart and a chart with numbers. Then fill in the blanks.

Shapes	How Many
△	
▭	
○	

Shapes	How Many
△	
▭	
○	

_____ more ▭ than ○   _____ fewer ○ than △

4 Read the clues.
Then color the dogs.

The blue dog is shortest.

The yellow dog is longer
than the red dog.

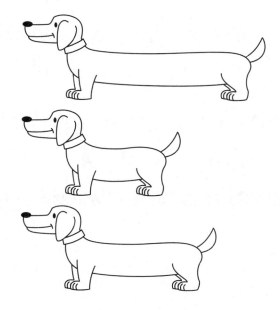

---

5 It is half past 7.

It is _____ minutes after _____ o'clock.

Show the time on these clocks.

 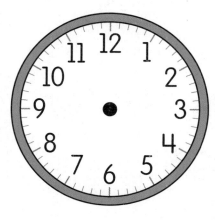

Put It Together

6 **Compare and measure.**

Color the longest pencil red.
Color the shortest pencil blue.

Measure the length of the longest pencil.
Use 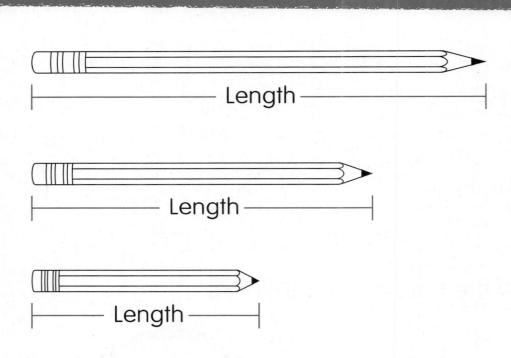 and ■.

Length

Length

Length

Length of longest pencil:

about _____ ■   about _____ ■